Parents and Marginalized Students

Parents and Marginalized Students
Essential Steps for Parents to Improve Schools

Gerard Giordano

ROWMAN & LITTLEFIELD
Lanham • Boulder • New York • London

Published by Rowman & Littlefield
An imprint of The Rowman & Littlefield Publishing Group, Inc.
4501 Forbes Boulevard, Suite 200, Lanham, Maryland 20706
www.rowman.com

86-90 Paul Street, London EC2A 4NE

Copyright © 2023 by Gerard Giordano

All rights reserved. No part of this book may be reproduced in any form or by any electronic or mechanical means, including information storage and retrieval systems, without written permission from the publisher, except by a reviewer who may quote passages in a review.

British Library Cataloguing in Publication Information Available

Library of Congress Cataloging-in-Publication Data
Library of Congress Cataloging-in-Publication DataNames: Giordano, Gerard, 1946- author.
  Title: Parents and marginalized students : essential steps for parents to
    improve schools / Gerard Giordano.
  Description: Lanham : Rowman & Littlefield, [2023] | Includes
    bibliographical references.
  Identifiers: LCCN 2023023950 (print) | LCCN 2023023951 (ebook) | ISBN
    9781475867718 (cloth) | ISBN 9781475867725 (paperback) | ISBN 9781475867732 (ebook)
  Subjects: LCSH: Parent-teacher relationships--United States. | Home and
    school--United States. | Children with social
    disabilities--Education--United States. | Marginality, Social--United
    States.
  Classification: LCC LC226.6 .G56 2023 (print) | LCC LC226.6 (ebook) | DDC
    371.19/20973--dc23/eng/20230824
  LC record available at https://lccn.loc.gov/2023023950
  LC ebook record available at https://lccn.loc.gov/2023023951

This book is for the many parents with whom I have collaborated. It originated from my conversations with them. I hope it encapsulates their enthusiasm and startlingly fresh insights.

Contents

Preface: Why Are Parents Upset about Marginalized Learners? . . . ix
Acknowledgment xiii
CHAPTER 1: Empowered Parents and Marginalized Students. 1
CHAPTER 2: Sports and Marginalized Students 13
CHAPTER 3: Dress Codes and Marginalized Students 23
CHAPTER 4: Emotional Supports and Marginalized Students 33
CHAPTER 5: Religious Policies and Marginalized Students 47
CHAPTER 6: Homeless Policies and Marginalized Students. 61
CHAPTER 7: LGBTQ Disclosure Policies and Marginalized Students 71
CHAPTER 8: High-Priced Instruction and Marginalized Students . .81
CHAPTER 9: Disability Policies and Marginalized Students. 93
CHAPTER 10: Medical Policies and Marginalized Students 105
CHAPTER 11: Military Service and Marginalized Students 115
CHAPTER 12: Immigration Status and Marginalized Students . . . 127
Bibliography 139
About the Author 185

Preface: Why Are Parents Upset about Marginalized Learners?

[Many of the minority parents at our school] feared their children would be marginalized.
—Parent Nikole Hannah-Jones, 2016

Students living in marginalized communities may feel targeted or unsafe.
—Virginia Department of Education, 2021

Marginalized [learners are] underserved, disregarded, ostracized, harassed, persecuted, [and] sidelined.
—The Charter for Compassion Organization, 2021

[One school board member insisted that he was] fighting for . . . marginalized communities.
—Journalist Christine Mai-Duc, 2022

Being nice [to marginalized learners] isn't enough.
—High School Teacher Nick Gehl, 2019

Preface: Why Are Parents Upset about Marginalized Learners?

Parents sent their children off to school. However, they kept their eyes on them. They wanted to know how they were doing academically.

The parents also wanted to know how their children were doing socially. They hoped that they would feel accepted. They had seen cases in which students had been singled out and ostracized because of gender, race, ethnicity, sexual orientation, disability, religion, immigration status, the language spoken at home, their family's income, their family's association with the armed services, or their family's attitudes toward medical issues.

The anxious parents went to the teachers. They told them that they worried that their children might be socially marginalized. They wanted their advice about how to protect them.

The teachers understood the parents' concerns about marginalization. However, they tried to reassure them. They explained that they were taking steps to reduce the chances that children would be marginalized. They gave examples.

- They had designated curricula and textbooks that stressed the social inclusion of all groups.
- They had introduced inclusive school policies for restrooms, athletics, sponsored events, extracurricular activities, and school attire.
- They had strictly disciplined students who ridiculed or bullied classmates.
- They had provided counseling to students who felt marginalized.

The teachers believed that the steps they were taking would influence children's social skills, self-confidence, and ethical values. However, they believed they also would influence their academic achievement. Teachers predicted that these efforts would serve as the foundation for happy and fulfilling experiences at school.

Many parents had confidence in the steps that the teachers were taking at school. In fact, they urged them to quicken their pace and expand their scale.

Preface: Why Are Parents Upset about Marginalized Learners?

Not all parents had confidence in the steps. Some were skeptical. The skeptics believed that the teachers were creating more problems than they were solving. They wanted to slow the pace of change and limit its scale.

The parents who supported the teachers were idealistic, articulate, and passionately committed to children. The skeptical parents shared these traits. Both groups refused to change their opinions or abandon their values.

The disputing parents shared another trait. They were convinced that they needed more members to prevail. They asked uncommitted parents to join their respective factions. They made the same pitch to uncommitted teachers, support staff, school administrators, and school board members. Some of them tried to recruit journalists and elected officials.

The disputing parents hoped to acquire greater influence. They shocked many people with the amount of media attention they attracted and the amount of political power they wielded.

Features

This book explores marginalization in schools and looks at the parent-led campaigns to neutralize marginalization.

The chapters in this book use the case method. They begin with a problem outside of the schools, follow with one inside the schools, and conclude with side-by-side analysis of the two problems. The idea is to help readers see how the solution to one problem can be the key to solving the other.

Series

This book is part of a series about the impact that parents have had on education. Two recent books in this series have focused on the impact they have had on school technology and school safety. This one concerns the impact they have had on marginalized students. The next book will focus on the impact they have had on school boards.

AUDIENCE

This book is intended for a general audience. It will be particularly useful to parents. However, it is also intended for teachers, school administrators, and all educational professionals.

Acknowledgment

This book is a tribute to my prescient editor—Tom Koerner. Tom, who detected the parents-in-schools movement when it was in its very early stages, suggested that I chronicle it in a series of books intended for a general audience.

Chapter 1

Empowered Parents and Marginalized Students

The role [of] parents... in the [Florida] public school system continues to gain attention.
—Journalist Jeffrey Solochek, 2021

[Florida's parents have the] right to direct the education and care of his or her minor child.
—Parents Bill of Rights, 2021

[Florida's] parental rights do not stop at the classroom door.
—Moms for Liberty Organization, 2022

[Florida's] school board meetings... [demonstrate that parental] craziness is real.
—United Teachers of Dade President Karla Hernández-Mats, 2022

Chapter 1

[After I read through some of Florida's current textbooks] I'm thinking to myself 2+2=4 not 2+2 and how does that make you feel.
—Florida Governor Ron DeSantis, 2022

[Florida's governor visited] Jacksonville to tout hand-picked school board candidates.
—Journalist Marilyn Parker, 2022

Twenty-five of the 30 school board [candidates] endorsed by [Florida's governor] won or advanced.
—Wall Street Journal Editorial Board, 2022

Florida legislators were concerned that crime victims were vulnerable because of the publicly accessible court information about them. They passed a law giving victims the right to sequester this information. They were surprised when police officers questioned whether the law applied to them.

The members of a Florida school board were concerned about a statewide regulation that restricted the teaching of Critical Race Theory (CRT). They assured their local teachers that they still had the right to design race-based instruction. They were surprised when parents questioned whether they had similar rights.

Empowered Police

Floridians wished to improve public safety. They detected multiple shortcomings. However, they disagreed about the reasons for the shortcomings.

Some Floridians attributed the shortcomings to unprofessional police officers. They demanded that officers wear body cameras, record their interactions with suspects, and then publicly share those video records. They asked their state legislators to codify these procedures.

Other Floridians did not blame the police for the decline in public safety. They highlighted dangers that the officers faced while they were making arrests. They noted that they routinely had to arrest suspects who were attacking them. They concluded that local law enforcement units should decide whether to release officers' body cam videos. They made this recommendation to their state legislators.

The legislators listened respectfully to their constituents' recommendations. However, they wished to shift the public safety debate away from police officers and criminal suspects. They wanted to focus on the victims of crime.

The legislators noted that Californians had enacted a victims' rights law in 2008. They wished to enact a similar law in Florida. Following the lead of the Californians, they wished to name their law after Marsy, who had been the victim in a heavily publicized crime.

The Florida legislators presented their proposal to voters in 2018. They argued that victims who testified against their assailants were not safe. They explained that they could be identified by their assailants from publicly accessible court records. They were pleased when voters authorized them to create their own version of Marsy's Law.

Enthusiasts
Victims of crime embraced Marsy's Law. Most of them were involved in situations that had been envisaged by Florida's voters. For example, they had provided evidence in court that had led to the conviction of criminals. They did not want associates of those criminals to harm them. They therefore used Marsy's Law to block the release of personally identifying information within court records.

On-duty police officers also invoked Marsy's Law. Most of them had been involved in situations that were different from those that the voters had envisaged.

The officers stated that they had been violently attacked while trying to arrest criminal suspects. They then provided their body cam videos to the courts. However, they did not want those videos released because they contained information that would endanger them and their families. They asked whether they could use Marsy's Law to block public release of those videos.

The legislators were caught off guard by the officers' request. They were not sure how to respond. They wondered how their constituents would feel about this request.

Constituents admitted that that they had not anticipated that officers would use Marsy's Law to suppress body cam videos. Nonetheless, they worried that officers and their families could be in peril if their body cam videos were released. Some of them concluded that the officers could invoke Marsy's Law.

Skeptics

Some Floridians were upset when on-duty police officers claimed that they should be able to invoke Marsy's Law. They did not consider them to be genuine crime victims.

The skeptics wanted police officers to release all bodycam videos. They acknowledged that the officers and their families might then be in danger. However, they argued that using Marsy's Law to protect them was unconstitutional.

Many journalists were extremely upset by the police officers who invoked Marsy's Law. They explained that they were depriving them of the videos that they needed to keep their readers and viewers informed.

The police officers were unprepared for the attacks by citizens and journalists. They turned for help to the leaders of local law enforcement agencies. However, they did not get the support for which they had hoped.

The police officers then turned to legislators. They asked them to clarify Marsy's Law. They asked if they had intended to protect all crime victims, including officers. Once again, they did not get the support for which they had hoped.

The police officers had been disappointed by local law enforcement agencies and the legislature. They turned to their union: the Florida Police Benevolent Association (FPBA). They asked its leaders for help.

The FPBA's leaders did not disappoint the officers. They contended that they were protected by Marsy's Law. They promised to defend them in court.

Empowered Parents

Florida's school board members managed the public schools in their communities. Those on the Duval County School Board managed the public schools in the City of Jacksonville.

The Duval County School Board members had powerful positions. They were responsible for more than one hundred thousand students and more than eight thousand teachers.

When candidates ran for the Duval County School Board, they did not have to win partisan primaries. They simply registered to compete in a general election. Although they did not have to win party primaries, they still had party loyalties. Some characterized themselves as Democrats; others characterized themselves as Republicans. At the beginning of 2022, four of them were Democrats and three were Republican. The two factions had different views about the schools.

The board members regularly held public meetings. They invited school personnel to them. They expected them to report on key issues. They listened carefully to them.

The board members also invited parents to their meetings. They wanted to give parents the chance to respond to the reports from school personnel. However, they noted that relatively few parents accepted these invitations. They probably knew the reason that they declined.

School Board meetings could be soporific. Writing in *The Atlantic*, Maureen Downey stated that she had been required to attend these meetings when she had been an educational journalist. She wrote that "I used to bring a book . . . to read during the lulls and the long presentations." However, she eventually noticed changes in the behaviors of parents and School Board members.

Downey chronicled some of the dramatic exchanges she witnessed. She then wondered whether she should "pack riot gear" to the meetings. Downey could very well have been talking about the meetings of the Duval School Board.

The Duval County School Board members shared a conviction that students should be aware of racism. They had textbooks packed with information on the topic. They assumed that teachers then elaborated on the topic.

Most board members were progressive-leaning. They believed that parents wanted teachers to underscore the historical examples of racism in their textbooks, supplement them with current examples of racism in their local community, and prepare their students to promote social justice.

The progressive faction of the Duval board members became nervous when the Florida State Board of Education expressed concerns about racially divisive learning materials and instruction. They were informed that the State Board had banned materials and instruction related to CRT.

The Duval board members were not completely surprised. They knew that some of the parents in their own community had been lobbying for a CRT ban. They also knew parents who had been opposed to the ban.

The pro-ban parents were enthusiastic about the State Board's stance. The anti-ban parents were apprehensive. Both groups had questions about the impact that the ban would have on local teachers. They directed their questions to local school leaders.

The school leaders indicated that the district's teachers had been following the curricula and standards prescribed by the Florida State Board of Education. They noted that CRT had not been a topic in those curricula or standards. They had told their teachers that they did not need to make any instructional changes.

Enthusiasts

The Duval parents had been focused on their children's health during the 2020 pandemic. They kept their children at home and watched them as they engaged in online instruction.

The Duval parents suddenly had opportunities that they had never had before. They could access digital learning materials, PowerPoint displays, blogs, and written assignments. They could virtually observe instruction, classroom discussions, and oral assignments. They witnessed everything that was transpiring in their children's classrooms.

The parents were intrigued when their children discussed the pervasive racism in their own community and in contemporary society. They believed that they were fully engaged. They concluded that that they were growing intellectually, emotionally, and socially. Many of them were pleased.

The parents were surprised when race-based topics from their children's social studies classes reemerged in their mathematics classes. However, some of them were not disconcerted. They may have recalled how their children had been frustrated by the abstract concepts in mathematics. They assumed that they would be more motivated and successful if those concepts were integrated with information about racism.

The parents did notice that the race-based mathematics materials were less rigorous than traditional materials. They still were supportive. They may have rationalized that a decline in rigor was a reasonable price to pay to advance social justice.

Skeptics

Parents of children in the Duval schools paid attention to the race-based instruction in online classes. They realized that it presented an unflattering view of America's society, economy, and government. Some of them questioned whether it was appropriate.

The skeptical parents met with teachers and school principals and asked if they would change their approach to race-based instruction. They were disappointed when they showed no interest in making changes.

The skeptical parents met with local school board members. They expressed their misgivings about the race-based instruction. They wished to collaboratively redesign it. They were frustrated after their offer was declined.

The frustrated parents eventually contacted the Florida State Board of Education and were pleased when it tried to help them. However, they discovered that it was no match for their local school board. They turned to their governor for assistance.

Governor Ron DeSantis listened to the frustrated parents. He assured them that they should be able to collaborate with their children's teachers about race-based instruction. Aware that they were at an impasse with local school boards, he made a practical suggestion.

The governor urged the frustrated parents to identify school board candidates who shared their views. He promised that he would then help their candidates get elected. He explained that he would endorse them, attend campaign events, and even transfer some of his own political funds to them.

Responding to Questions about Contentious Issues

This section focuses on the preceding two cases. The first case involved legislators in Florida.

The legislators were concerned about the rights of crime victims. However, they discovered that their constituents disagreed among themselves about those rights.

The legislators looked for a way to unite constituents with diverse views. They hoped that they could bring constituents together with a law to protect crime victims who testified against their assailants in court.

The legislators noted that victims who testified against their assailants feared they would be attacked in retaliation. These victims explained that their personal information was contained in publicly accessible court records. They argued for a special law to sequester this information. They wished to call it Marsy's Law.

The legislators investigated how voters felt about this proposal. They were pleased that most of them supported it. They eagerly enacted the new law.

The legislators later wondered how the new law was being used. They were not surprised that crime victims who testified against assailants were employing the law to conceal their identities. However, they were surprised that on-duty police officers were employing it.

The officers believed that they were crime victims when they were attacked by the persons whom they were trying to arrest. They noted that the body cam videos that they submitted in court contained information about their identities. They worried that this information could lead to retaliatory attacks against them and their families if it were publicly accessible.

The officers asked the legislators to clarify their rights under Marsy's Law. When they did not obtain this clarification, they turned to the leaders of their local law enforcement agencies for assistance. When they were still frustrated, they turned to the leaders of the Florida Fraternal Order of Police.

While the first case in this chapter concerned legislators, the next one focused on the board members for the Duval Public Schools. These board members were responsible for instruction.

The board members represented constituents with extremely different views about instruction. They wished to please as many as they could.

All of the board members believed that the teachers should provide race-based instruction. However, they disagreed about how the teachers should proceed. The majority encouraged the teachers to use their professional discretion when designing this instruction. The minority encouraged them to make sure that the parents had a role in designing the instruction.

Parents learned that the majority of the school board members had prevailed. Some of them were pleased. They believed that the board's approach to race-based instruction would foster social justice.

Not all parents supported the majority's approach. They were particularly opposed to strand of instruction that relied on CRT. Some of them worried that CRT was socially divisive.

The disgruntled parents asked the local school board members to reconsider their stance. However, they could not change their minds. They therefore turned to the Florida State Board of Education. They asked it to enact a statewide ban on CRT-based instruction, which they judged to be particularly divisive. They were pleased when the State Board enacted this ban.

The disgruntled parents hoped that the state ban on CRT instruction would be effective. However, they soon concluded that it was having a minimal impact in the Duval schools.

The members of the displeased faction looked for another ally. This time they turned to their governor. They were jubilant when he took their side and presented them with a proposal. He would help them oust their local school board members and replace them with new ones.

The following questions will assist you if you are going through this book on your own. They provide opportunities like those you would have in a college class where the professor uses the case method and help if you are in an actual class using this approach.

Question 1: How Did Florida Legislators Handle Crime Victims Who Were Vulnerable to Retaliation?

Florida legislators realized that crime victims who testified in court against assailants were vulnerable to retaliation. They therefore enacted Marsy's Law, which gave them the right to sequester personal information from publicly accessible court records.

How did different groups in Florida respond to the legislators? Focus on two groups: police officers and state residents.

Did the police officers have low confidence, moderate confidence, or high confidence in the way that the legislators were behaving? How did state residents feel? Explain the basis for your answers.

When answering these questions, as well as those that follow, you can rely on the information in this chapter. You might also use some of the sources identified in the references at the back of this book. If you are reading this chapter with a group, talk about the best way to answer the questions.

Question 2: How Did Florida Legislators Handle Police Officers Who Were Vulnerable to Retaliation?

Florida legislators discovered that police officers were vulnerable to retaliation from the suspects that they had arrested. The legislators seemed nonplussed when the officers asked if Marsy's Law gave them the right to sequester the personal information contained in publicly accessible body cam videos. They took no action.

How did different groups in Florida respond to the legislators? Focus on two groups: police officers and state residents.

Did the police officers have low confidence, moderate confidence, or high confidence in the way that the legislators were behaving? How did the state residents feel? Explain the basis for your answers.

Question 3: How Did the Florida School Board Handle Race-Based Instruction?

The Duval County School Board's members believed that race-based instruction enriched learning and advanced social justice. They assured classroom teachers that they had the right to design and implement this instruction.

How did diverse groups respond to school board members? Focus on two groups: teachers and parents.

Did the teachers have low confidence, moderate confidence, or high confidence in the way the School Board members were behaving? How did the parents feel? Explain the basis for your answers.

Question 4: How Did the Florida School Board Handle Race-Based Instruction after a Statewide CRT Ban?

The Duval County School Board's members were advised of a statewide ban on CRT in the schools. They assured local teachers that this ban did not compromise their right to design and implement race-based instruction. They seemed perplexed when parents asked if they had this right. No action was taken.

How did diverse groups respond to the School Board members? Focus on two groups: teachers and parents.

Did the teachers have low confidence, moderate confidence, or high confidence in the way that the School Board members were behaving? How did the parents feel? Explain the basis for your answers.

Summary

Florida legislators were concerned because personal information about crime victims was accessible in publicly accessible court records. They passed a law giving victims the right to sequester this information. They seemed surprised and confused when police officers questioned whether they had the same right.

The members of a local School Board were concerned about a statewide ban on CRT instruction in Florida. They assured teachers that they still had the right to design race-based instruction. They seemed surprised and confused when parents questioned whether they had similar rights.

Chapter 2

Sports and Marginalized Students

An average of 1.8% of high school students identify as transgender.
  —CDC Researcher Michelle Johns, 2019

Transgender . . . youth are . . . at higher risk for . . . suicide because of bullying, discrimination, and rejection.
  —Trevor Anti-Suicide Project CEO Amit Paley, 2021

Students should have the opportunity to participate in interscholastic athletics in a manner that is consistent with their gender identity.
  —Florida High School Athletic Association, 2022

It is discriminatory to force [girls] to compete against [transgender girls who were born as] biological males.
  —Florida Governor Ron DeSantis, 2021

[Scholastic] sports designated for females, women, or girls may not be open to students of the male sex . . . [as defined on their] official birth certificate.
  —Florida Fairness in Women's Sports Act, 2022

Chapter 2

The stated intent of [Florida Fairness in Women's Sports Act] is to maintain opportunities for female athletes.
—Attorney Kayla Platt Rady, 2021

[Laws restricting transgender athletes] are harassing girls who happen to not look like a Barbie doll and want to play sports.
—Human Rights Campaign Counsel Cathryn Oakley, 2021

Executives at Facebook invited all users to their website. However, they later changed their minds. They explained that they had not fully considered the consequences of allowing dangerous individuals to access their site.

Florida's elected officials invited all schoolgirls to compete on girls' sports teams. However, they later changed their minds. They explained that they had not fully considered the consequences of allowing transgender girls to compete.

Banning Facebook Users

Many students had applied for admittance to Harvard in 2004. Those who were accepted could not have been more excited. They informed the admissions staff that they would attend.

The new students were even more excited after they set foot on the Harvard University campus. They eagerly attended the orientation sessions that the admissions staff had arranged for them.

The students received a campus map, an index of campus organizations, a list of services, and a bulletin with the classes in which they could register. However, many of them doubted that they would ever use these items. They therefore immediately discarded them

The students received one more item: a directory with names and photos of classmates. They referred to this directory as the campus "Facebook." Anticipating that they would use this item, they kept it.

Mark Zuckerberg was a member of the 2004 class. He and several of his classmates were struck by the student directory. They did not doubt that it was useful. However, they believed that it could be much more useful.

Zuckerberg and his colleagues digitized Facebook. They then loaded the files onto a website and gave them a new name—*Face Mash*.

Zuckerberg allowed Harvard's students to post texts, photos, and videos on *Face Mash*. He also allowed them to befriend classmates and communicate through the website. He provided these services at no charge.

Face Mash went online in 2004. However, it soon reverted to its former name—*Facebook*.

Harvard's Facebook website quickly spread to other campuses. It then became available to the general public. In less than fifteen years, it became available worldwide. It was an immense success.

High-powered executives were recruited for Facebook. They were responsible for managing the staff and the operations of this increasingly complex media company.

The executives initially had used the name *Facebook* to identify their company as well as their website. However, they later reorganized the company as a corporation and changed its name to *Meta Platforms*.

The executives recognized the features that had made Facebook so popular. They vowed to retain them.

- They welcomed virtually all users to their website.
- They charged them no fees.
- They allowed them to communicate with each other.
- They allowed them to post personal information.
- They guaranteed them that their personal information would not be distributed to marketers.
- They guaranteed them that the website would maintain politically unbiased attitudes toward local, national, and international news.

The Facebook executives had legions of enthusiastic admirers. However, they also had critics.

CHAPTER 2

The critics recognized the enormous power that the Facebook executives had acquired. They disapproved of the way that they were wielding it. They were particularly critical of the policy that allowed open access to the website. They believed that the executives should ban anyone who had attempted to post fake information.

The executives took steps to appease these critics. They hired censors to locate inaccurate information and label it as fake.

The executives were pleased with the job that the censors were doing. They soon gave them an additional job. They directed them to keep tabs on any individuals who had posted fake information and then blacklist them. They told them to be especially alert for individuals who were threats to their communities.

Enthusiasts
The Facebook executives wondered how people were reacting to the changes that they had made to their policies. They were especially interested in elected government officials, who had demanded that the executives do a better job of regulating their website.

Some elected officials expressed enthusiasm for the changes. They especially liked the blacklist. However, they demanded more details. They wanted to know the names of the people who were on the blacklist.

Some elected officials had fumed after President Donald Trump made highly popular but inaccurate posts on Facebook. They wanted to know whether he was on the blacklist.

Some Facebook users agreed with the anti-Trump elected officials. They were convinced that Trump had made posts that were patently bogus and potentially dangerous. They hoped that the executives would blacklist him.

The Facebook executives did place Trump on their blacklist. They stated that they took this step to prevent him from harming the country.

Skeptics
The Facebook executives had taken steps to improve their website. However, they had not placated their most persistent critics. These critics wished to question the website censors.

The Facebook censors candidly answered the questions that were posed to them. Some of them admitted that they had not been able to do their jobs. They gave examples.

The censors had attempted to block Facebook content that promoted eating disorders, depression, insecurity, and loneliness. They disclosed that they had been scolded because this content was designed to entice young females to the website.

The censors noted that Facebook had a secret whitelist. They noted that the people on this list, who had large social followings, were off-limits to censors.

The critics were impressed by the disclosures that they obtained from the Facebook censors. They accused the corporation's executives of behaving no more ethically than they had before the website changes had been made.

Banning Transgender Athletes

Florida's elected officials were responsible for school academics. However, they typically did not get involved. They delegated most of their academic responsibilities to the Florida Commissioner of Education, the Florida Board of Education, and the Florida Department of Education.

Florida's elected officials were responsible for school sports as well as school academics. In this, too, they tried to remain uninvolved. They delegated these responsibilities to athletic associations.

The elected officials depended heavily on the Florida High School Athletic Association. They appreciated its decisions about participant eligibility, student safety, competition, and fairness in high school sports.

The elected officials appreciated the Florida High School Athletic Association for still another reason. They noted that it consulted with parents before making important decisions. They assumed that the parents were grateful.

The parents were grateful. They cared deeply about sports. They had observed the enormous influence that participation in school sports had on their children's physical, social, cognitive, and emotional development. Many of them hoped that participation in school sports might lead

CHAPTER 2

to college scholarships or even contracts with professional teams for their kids.

The parents expected full student participation in school sports. They generally were pleased. They discerned ample opportunities for girls and boys. They gave credit to the Florida High School Athletic Association for monitoring these opportunities.

The parents initially had few concerns about the eligibility criteria for participating in school sports. However, some of them later changed their minds.

The parents of transgender daughters had concerns. They wanted their daughters to have the same opportunities as other girls. They therefore had encouraged them to try out for girls' teams. They were distressed when they were blocked by coaches.

The parents of transgender daughters protested to the coaches. Sometimes they changed the coaches' minds. When they could not, they appealed to school principals. When they still encountered resistance, they moved on to district athletic directors, superintendents, and local boards of education.

Some of these disgruntled parents met with the Florida High School Athletic Association. They were excited after this organization expressed support for transgender girls to play on girls' teams. However, they were frustrated when their daughters were still blocked by school personnel.

These parents eventually went to journalists, described their daughters' plight and tried to stir up public outrage.

In 2021, parents with transgender daughters asked Florida's legislators and governor to guarantee that their daughters could play on girls' teams. They told them that this request had the support of the Florida High School Athletic Association, journalists, and many members of the public.

The disgruntled parents waited for the elected officials to respond to their request. They were devastated when they learned their decision: the officials barred transgender girls from playing on girls' teams at school.

The disgruntled parents publicly scolded the officials. They stated that they were misinformed about transgender girls. Some went further and called them bigots.

The elected officials stated that they genuinely sympathized with the transgender girls and their parents. They added that they also understood the reason for the request. Nonetheless, they could not grant their request. The officials explained that transgender girls had been born with male bodies; they were sure that they had so much of a physical advantage that they would be unbeatable in girls' sports.

Enthusiasts

After Florida's elected officials enacted the transgender school sports ban, they paid attention to how students were reacting. They were extremely interested in them because the ban affected them directly.

The transgender girls who wished to compete on girls' teams were upset. Many of their non-transgender classmates, especially those in high school, also were upset. However, not all students were upset. Some of them supported the ban.

The students who supported the ban had competed against transgender girls at sports events. They had grumbled about the physical advantages of these girls.

The students who supported the ban complained privately to peers, parents, teachers, and coaches. However, some of them complained publicly to journalists and newscasters.

Many parents also supported the ban. They stated that transgender girls should have opportunities for full social inclusion but insisted that social inclusion and athletic fairness were separate issues.

Skeptics

Transgender schoolgirls had been playing on girls' teams throughout Florida. Needless to say, they were devastated when they learned that a statewide ban would keep them off their teams.

Florida's transgender schoolgirls envied their peers who lived in states without bans. They noted that those in California had a law protecting the athletic rights of transgender schoolgirls.

Many non-transgender high school students sympathized with their transgender classmates. They criticized the elected officials who were responsible for the ban and wondered if they had ulterior motives for enacting it.

The skeptical students worried that some members of the pro-ban group had little interest in promoting athletic fairness. They suspected that they were motivated by bias against classmates who were LGBTIQQ (Lesbian, Gay, Bisexual, Transgender, Intersex, Queer, or Questioning).

The parents of transgender girls hotly contested the ban. They dreaded the emotional and psychological harm that it could cause. They were assisted by parents who did not have transgender daughters but who detected numerous negative effects and few benefits.

The skeptical parents acknowledged that some transgender girls had dominated high school sports. However, they contended that their number had been relatively low. They characterized the ban as a heavy-handed response to an extremely small problem.

Responding to Questions about Restrictions

Four questions have been placed in this section. They focus on the preceding two case studies.

The first case study centered on the executives at Facebook. These executives initially had allowed unrestricted access to their website. They believed that users supported this policy.

The executives later realized that many users did not support unrestricted access. They discovered that they were concerned about people who were posting fake or dangerous information.

The executives modified their user policy. They barred dangerous people from using Facebook.

The executives assumed that their decision would be highly popular. However, they were surprised by its complex consequences.

While the first case study centered on Facebook executives, the next one centered on elected officials in Florida. These officials had multiple responsibilities, including those pertaining to school sports.

The elected officials had delegated their responsibilities for school sports to their state's athletic associations. They did not intervene when these associations recommended unrestricted participation. They assumed that parents were supportive.

The elected officials later realized that many parents did not support unrestricted participation. These parents had concerns that transgender girls who joined girls' teams and competed at girls' sporting events would dominate those events.

Florida's elected officials decided that they needed to take personal control of school sports. They enacted a law that barred transgender girls from playing on girls' teams.

The elected officials assumed that their decision would be highly popular. However, they were surprised by its complex consequences.

The following questions will assist you if you are going through this book on your own. They provide opportunities like those you would have in a college class where the professor uses the case method and help if you are in an actual class using this approach.

Question 1: Why Did Executives Initially Allow Unrestricted Access to Facebook?

Executives at Facebook allowed unrestricted access to their website. They calculated that user satisfaction would increase as a result.

How did different groups respond to the executives? Focus on two groups: website users and elected officials.

Did the users have low confidence, moderate confidence, or high confidence in the way that the executives were behaving? How did elected officials feel? Explain the basis for your answers.

When answering these questions, as well as those that follow, you can rely on the information in this chapter. You might also use some of the sources that are identified in the references at the back of the book. If you are reading this chapter with a group, talk about the best way to answer the questions.

Question 2: Why Did the Executives Later Restrict Access to Facebook?

Executives at Facebook believed that user satisfaction was decreasing. They attributed the decline to concerns about fake or dangerous posts on their website. They therefore restricted access.

How did different groups respond to the executives? Focus on two groups: website users and elected officials.

Did the users have low confidence, moderate confidence, or high confidence in the way that the executives were behaving? How did elected officials feel? Explain the basis for your answers.

Question 3: Why Did Florida's Elected Officials Initially Allow Unrestricted Participation in Girls' School Sports?

Elected officials in Florida allowed unrestricted participation in girls' school sports. They calculated that public satisfaction would increase as a result.

How did diverse groups respond to the elected officials? Focus on two groups: students and parents.

Did the students have low confidence, moderate confidence, or high confidence in the way that the elected officials were behaving? How did the parents feel? Explain the basis for your answers.

Question 4: Why Did Florida's Elected Officials Later Restrict Participation in Girls' School Sports?

Elected officials in Florida believed that public satisfaction with girls' school sports was decreasing. They attributed the decline to concerns about the transgender girls who dominated some sports. They therefore restricted transgender girls' participation.

How did diverse groups respond to the elected officials? Focus on two groups: students and parents.

Did the students have low confidence, moderate confidence, or high confidence in the way that the elected officials were behaving? How did the parents feel? Explain the basis for your answers.

Summary

Executives at Facebook initially invited all users to their site. However, they later blocked dangerous individuals out of concern for safety.

Elected officials in Florida initially invited all schoolgirls to compete on girls' sports teams. However, they later blocked transgender girls out of concern for fairness.

CHAPTER 3

Dress Codes and Marginalized Students

[Our school's] dress code is . . . helping students learn [an employment] skill . . . linked to attire.
—GRESHAM-BARLOW SCHOOLS, 2022

Principals shall interpret and enforce . . . dress codes.
—ALBUQUERQUE PUBLIC SCHOOLS, 2022

Dresses may be worn, provided they are not distracting, as determined by the school administration.
—DUVAL COUNTY PUBLIC SCHOOLS, 2022

Girls at my high school just got dress coded for the dumbest reasons, like ripped jeans or a rip too high.
—STUDENT JISHA JOSEPH, 2021

Many [dress codes] target girls, and especially black girls, by regulating skirt length and headwraps.
—NATIONAL WOMEN'S LAW CENTER, 2018

Chapter 3

Girls with bigger bodies are disproportionately disciplined for dress code violations.
—Former Teacher NaChé Thompson, 2019

I have been dress coded multiple times at school and . . . told it was because [my skin] was distracting.
—Anonymous High School Student, 2022

What does it say to a 10-year-old when her body is routinely measured and critiqued?
—Mental Health Therapists Amy Bryant and Janie Mardis, 2021

Sports officials established dress codes for elite beach handball players. They prescribed one for males and a separate one for females. They seemed surprised by complaints that the female code was unfair.

Educational administrators established dress codes for high school students. They prescribed one for males and a separate one for females. They seemed surprised by complaints that the female code was unfair.

Dress Codes for Athletes

The officials at the International Handball Federation (IHF) planned high-profile tournaments. They had to consider the interests of multiple groups.

The officials had to make sure that fans would be attracted to events and able to attend. They had to take steps so that the media would film events and that viewers would watch them. They had to contact journalists to publicize and promote their events. They had to arrange for top-tier athletes to participate. They had to negotiate with sponsors to underwrite the costs for events.

The officials traditionally arranged European team handball tournaments on indoor hard-floored courts. They had anticipated that these venues would remain popular indefinitely. However, they had miscalculated. They discovered that fans and viewers were losing interest in the traditional tournaments. They concluded that they would have to make changes.

The officials had been transitioning to a new style of handball event—beach handball. They made arrangements for the athletes to play this type of handball outdoors in sand-covered settings. They were pleased when fans and viewers became excited about the new format.

The officials had to organize beach handball tournaments that would prepare players for the 2020 Summer Olympics. They directed their organization's regional groups to arrange the tournaments on six continents.

The officials in the European Handball Federation (EHF) listened carefully to their colleagues at the IHF. They were then ready to proceed.

The EHF officials informed athletes of the dates and locations for beach handball tournaments. They also specified the type of clothing that they should wear at them.

Beach handballers traditionally competed in poolside attire. The men had worn t-shirts and shorts. The women had worn crop tops and bikini bottoms.

The officials told the participants that they would continue to wear their traditional outfits at the pre-Olympics tournaments. They made it clear to them that they would incur fines if they did not comply.

Enthusiasts

The EHF officials believed that they had devised a winning formula for handball events. They credited this formula for the increasing popularity of beach handball. They did not wish to tamper with it by changing the dress code. Nonetheless, they were eager to see how groups would react to their decision to retain their traditional dress code.

The officials kept an eye on the fans. They noted that they had enjoyed watching athletes participate in a sport with a beach-themed culture. They were relieved when some of them thanked the officials for preserving that culture.

The officials also kept an eye on beach handball sponsors. They were aware that these sponsors had contracts with the athletes. They were eager to see their reaction to the dress code.

CHAPTER 3

The sponsors expected the athletes to endorse a full range of sporting products, including clothing. They made sure that the logos of their firms were displayed prominently on the clothing.

The sponsors believed that the fans were impressed when they saw women athletes wearing bathing suits from their firms. They were relieved that they would continue to see them. They were enthusiastic about the dress code.

The EHF officials had one more group to which they were attentive. They focused on the athletes. They believed that the athletes appreciated their efforts to create publicity for them. They anticipated that they would view the dress code as one more effort on their behalf.

Many athletes were supportive of the officials. They had complied with their decisions about clothing for years. They agreed with the officials that their current outfits contributed to their enormous popularity. They were enthusiastic about the dress code.

Skeptics

Not all of the handballers were enthusiastic about EHF's athletic dress codes. The female athletes from Norway objected to them.

The Norwegian women handballers did not approve of crop tops. They preferred tank tops. They were especially disdainful of bikini bottoms. They preferred shorts.

The Norwegian team members asked the EHF officials to allow them to use their discretion about how they dressed. They urged them to copy the Olympics officials, who were permitting each country to determine the outfits that their athletes would wear during events.

The Norwegian women handballers wanted to compete in clothing that they considered to be functional and comfortable. They conceded that crop tops and bikini bottoms were functional and relatively comfortable. However, they felt that they also were sexually exploitative. For this reason, they preferred tank tops and shorts.

The EHF officials disagreed with the Norwegian team members. They warned them that they would be fined if they violated the official dress code.

The Norwegian team members appealed to fellow athletes for support. They were gratified when many female athletes, including those who intended to wear crop tops and bikini bottoms during competitions, urged the EHF officials to relax their dress code. They also received support from many male athletes.

The Norwegians hoped that journalists and politicians would support them. They were not disappointed. Both groups exerted enormous pressure on the intransigent EHF officials.

Dress Codes for Students

Educational administrators advised students how to dress. Some of them gave precise advice. For example, they told them to wear uniforms.

Most administrators did not require their students to wear uniforms. In fact, they gave them relatively few details about how to dress. They instead gave them rules about how they should avoid dressing.

The administrators referred to these rules as *dress codes*. They frequently had a dress code that prohibited males from wearing pants that sagged.

The administrators were nervous about enforcing the sagging pants prohibition. They realized that many of the boys with sagging pants were African American. When they had attempted to confront and penalize offenders, those boys had accused them of racial discrimination. As a result, they had backed off.

The administrators realized that the female students were unlikely to wear sagging pants. They therefore devised separate dress codes for them.

The administrators at the Socorro Independent School District in El Paso noted that female students were wearing skimpy skirts and shorts. They were ready to confront and penalize these students.

The Socorro administrators warned female students that they would be conducting a skimpy skirts and shorts test. They explained that they would be administering it in hallways and classrooms. They strongly advised students to self-administer the skimpy skirts and shorts test before they came to school.

The students were to stand with their arms hanging at their sides. They were to then measure whether their skirts or shorts extended beyond their fingertips. They could wear the outfit if it passed this test. They could not wear it if it failed. Those who failed would be sent home to change their clothes.

The female students had no confidence in the dress code. They were aware that their male classmates had been able to evade dress code penalties by accusing their school administrators of racial bias. They made a similar accusation. However, they accused the administrators of gender bias.

The female students hoped that their accusation would cause the administrators to pause, reevaluate their dress codes, and penalize them less frequently. They were disappointed when it did not.

Enthusiasts

The educational administrators were excited about their dress codes. They were eager to see how people were reacting to them.

The educational administrators kept watch on their teachers. After all, they depended on them to enforce the codes. They realized that they had to be supportive, or the codes would languish.

The teachers had multiple responsibilities. Nonetheless, they considered instruction to be their primary responsibility. They assumed that they would be more successful as instructors if students paid greater attention to them rather than other students.

The teachers had been on the lookout for ways to reduce classroom distractions. Some of them viewed dress codes as potent strategies. They professed confidence in them and pledged to enforce them.

Some of the teachers had another reason for supporting dress codes. They noted that students had worn garments with insignias that had antagonized gang members in their schools. They believed some of them had worn this clothing deliberately while others had worn it inadvertently. They believed that violent incidents would be reduced if all students followed dress codes that restricted clothing with gang insignias.

The administrators were pleased by the teachers who endorsed their dress codes. They hoped that parents would endorse them as well. They carefully monitored the parents' reactions.

Parents worried that their children would be picked on, belittled, and marginalized if they did not wear trendy outfits. They believed that dress codes would reduce the pressure to wear this clothing. These parents supported the codes.

Some parents disapproved of clothing that they considered to be immodest. They favored codes that banned these clothes. They enthusiastically supported the codes.

Skeptics
The educational administrators were pleased that some parents supported their dress codes. However, they quickly realized that many did not.

The non-supportive parents were annoyed at the educators because of the erratic manner in which they were enforcing dress codes. They noted that they were singling out a disproportionately high number of female students for violations.

A group of parents in a Florida school district believed that educators had made dress codes into sources of stress for their daughters. They gave an example to underscore this allegation.

One person in that Florida school district had digitally retouched the clothing of female students in eighty yearbook photos. She had explained that she had made these alternations so that the students would appear more modest.

The students with altered yearbook photos were upset. They appealed to their parents, who were also upset.

Female students throughout Florida sympathized with these students. They were sure that they had been the victims of gender bias. They gave details about similar incidents at their own schools.

The female students hoped that journalists and politicians would support them. They were not disappointed. Both groups exerted enormous pressure on educators.

RESPONDING TO QUESTIONS ABOUT DRESS CODES
This section focuses on the preceding two cases. The first case concerned the athletic officials who regulated beach handball tournaments.

Chapter 3

These officials specified regulations that the athletes were to follow during tournaments. They made sure to specify dress codes.

The officials established a dress code for the male athletes. They ran into no problems with it.

The officials established a dress code for female athletes that was quite different than that for the males. They immediately ran into a problem: The female athletes felt that their dress code was sexually exploitative.

While the first case in this chapter concerned athletic officials, the next one focused on educational administrators. The administrators were responsible for student dress codes.

The administrators specified dress codes for male students. They ran into hardly any problems.

The administrators established dress codes for female students that were quite different than those for male students. They immediately into a problem: Female students felt that their dress codes were gender biased.

The following questions will assist you if you are going through this book on your own. They provide opportunities like those you would have in a college class where the professor uses the case method and help if you are in an actual class using this approach.

Question 1: How Did Athletic Officials Handle Dress Codes for Male Handballers?

Athletic officials specified the attire that male athletes should wear during beach handball tournaments. They prescribed relatively modest outfits: t-shirts and shorts. They then penalized few male athletes for violating this dress code.

How did different groups respond to the officials? Focus on two groups: sponsors and athletes.

Did the sponsors have low confidence, moderate confidence, or high confidence in the way that the officials were behaving? How did the athletes feel? Explain the basis for your answers.

When answering these questions, as well as those that follow, you can rely on the information in this chapter. You might also use on some of the sources that are identified in the references at the back of the book.

If you are reading this chapter with a group, talk about the best way to answer the questions.

Question 2: How Did Athletic Officials Handle Dress Codes for Female Handballers?

Athletic officials specified the attire in which female athletes should compete during beach handball tournaments. They prescribed revealing outfits: crop tops and bikini bottoms. They then penalized numerous female athletes for violating this dress code.

How did different groups respond to the officials? Focus on two groups: sponsors and athletes.

Did the sponsors have low confidence, moderate confidence, or high confidence in the way that the officials were behaving? How did the athletes feel? Explain the basis for your answers.

Question 3: How Did Educational Administrators Handle Dress Codes for Male Students?

Educational administrators specified the attire in which male students should dress. They made the dress codes gender-specific. They then penalized few males for violating the codes.

How did diverse groups respond to these administrators? Focus on two groups: teachers and students.

Did the teachers have low confidence, moderate confidence, or high confidence in the way that the administrators were behaving? How did the students feel? Explain the basis for your answers.

Question 4: How Did Educational Administrators Handle Dress Codes for Female Students?

Educational administrators specified the attire in which female students should dress. They made the dress codes gender-specific. They then penalized numerous females for violating the codes.

How did diverse groups respond to these administrators? Focus on two groups: teachers and students.

Did the teachers have low confidence, moderate confidence, or high confidence in the way that the administrators were behaving? How did the students feel? Explain the basis for your answers.

Summary

Sports officials established dress codes for the competitors at beach handball tournaments. They prescribed modest outfits for males and revealing outfits for females. Although they insisted that they fairly enforced the two codes, they received complaints that female athletes were being unfairly singled out and penalized.

Educational administrators established dress codes for their students. They used one code for males and a different one for females. Although they insisted that they fairly enforced the two codes, they received complaints that female students were being unfairly singled out and penalized.

Chapter 4

Emotional Supports and Marginalized Students

[Chicago's current school restroom policy is that] accommodations should be assessed on a case-by-case basis.
—Chicago Public Schools, 2015

[We have a new school restroom policy that] is a big step forward for gender equity.
—Chicago Public Schools, 2021

Chicago Public Schools are . . . erasing single-sex spaces for males and females.
—Journalist Nicole Russell, 2021

Gender-neutral restroom signs [have been] posted at Chicago public schools.
—Journalist Brooke Migdon, 2021

CHAPTER 4

[Our new school restroom policy enables students] to use bathrooms without threat of violence or harassment.
—CHICAGO PUBLIC SCHOOLS SEXUAL HEALTH SPECIALIST DERRICK LITTLE, 2021

[How does the new school restroom policy] ensure no boy will try to peek at [my daughter] while she is in a stall?
—UNIDENTIFIED CHICAGO PARENT, 2021

EXECUTIVES AT DELTA AIRLINES PLACED STRICT RESTRICTIONS ON passengers during the COVID-19 pandemic. However, they worried that they were making some passengers anxious about flying. They tried to ease their anxiety by allowing them to bring emotional support animals on flights. They were surprised by the complex consequences.

Educational administrators in Chicago designated gender-specific school restrooms. However, they worried that they were making some students anxious about using them. They tried to ease their anxiety by allowing them to use gender-neutral restrooms. They were surprised by the complex consequences.

EASING PASSENGER ANXIETY ON FLIGHTS

Delta Airlines is known for its size. It has over 800 aircraft. It sends them to hundreds of destinations daily.

Delta is also known for its management. It recruits top-notch professionals into its ranks. It has been regularly honored as one of the best managed corporations in the travel industry.

Delta is known for another important attribute. It is remarkably profitable. For a long stretch, Delta generated more than $45 billion a year.

The executives at Delta were proud of the ways that passengers responded to their airline. They noted that passengers lauded its safety, reliability, convenience, comfort, customer service, and value.

The executives depended heavily on their airline's reputation to lure customers. They also depended on marketers. However, they used the marketers to a lesser extent than their competitors. They paid commercial marketers less than $100 million a year, which was a relatively small amount for such a huge business.

The executives hoped that Delta would continue to lure passengers at the same pace that it had for years. However, they became less optimistic during the COVID-19 pandemic. They realized that the demand for their flights was shrinking. Delta executives calculated that their profits were also shrinking. They were startled when their profits shrank by 50 percent in 2020.

Delta had continued to operate flights during the pandemic. However, they had taken steps to keep their flight crews and passengers safe. For example, they imposed strict safety restrictions.

Delta's staff wore facemasks. They then gave passengers facemasks before they boarded. They followed up by handing them packets of disinfectants once they were onboard. They assigned them seats that were distanced from those of fellow passengers. They did not offer them food or beverage services.

The executives had confidence in Delta's safety measures. They were sure that these measures would protect passengers from the virus. However, they realized that these measures would also remind them of the deadly risks that they were taking on flights.

The executives wished to prod passengers to comply with their safety measures. They simultaneously wished to prod them to continue flying. They asked their marketers how to handle these conflicting messages.

The marketers had a history of conveying persuasive messages on behalf of Delta. They had placed these messages on television, on billboards, in magazines, and online. They intended to continue using these media.

The marketers historically had targeted messages at passengers who were concerned about convenience, efficiency, and reliability. They wish to continue sending messages to these passengers. However, they wished to target messages to some additional groups. For example, they wished to target passengers who wished to spend less for basic transportation as well as those who were willing to spend more for luxury perks.

Chapter 4

The marketers had one more suggestion. They pointed out that Delta historically had taken steps to comfort people who had an intense psychological fear of flying. They noted that it had used carefully selected language to explain the safety steps that these passengers should take in an emergency. They believed that it could build on this experience to comfort people who had an intense psychological fear of contracting the virus.

The marketers searched for strategies with which to entice people who feared that they would contract COVID-19 on planes. They came up with a suggestion. They assumed that some of these fearful people had special relationships with their pets. They hoped to entice them by taking advantage of those relationships.

The marketers reviewed Delta's history of handling animals on flights. They noted that it had separated the animals from their owners, placed them in cages, and then transported them in cargo sections. They wanted to make it easy for these animals to travel next to their owners.

Delta already permitted some animals to fly with passengers in the cabins of flights. As examples, it permitted dogs that assisted persons with low vision, seizures, some medical conditions, and psychiatric issues.

The marketers praised the Delta executives for making animal-centered concessions. However, they urged them to make even more.

The marketers explained that psychiatric service dogs (PSDs) had been accompanying Delta passengers with medically diagnosed fear of flying. They suggested that personal pets accompany passengers who had a fear of contracting COVID. They explained that the executives could treat these pets, which would not qualify as PSDs, as emotional support animals (ESAs).

The executives were intrigued by this proposal. They agreed that Delta passengers should be permitted to bring their pets. However, they would require that they obtain letters attesting that their pets would reduce anxiety. They took this step to make sure that the pet lovers did not overwhelm their fellow passengers.

Enthusiasts

Delta's executives were eager to see how key groups responded to their new animals-on-planes policy. They were especially eager to see how the U.S. Department of Transportation (USDOT) responded.

The USDOT staff reviewed policies affecting animals on planes. During their reviews, they made sure that the animals, passengers, and airline staff would be safe. After they had reviewed the new Delta policy, they approved it.

The executives were pleased after they received approval from the USDOT. However, they wished to see the response from passengers. They focused on passengers with special anxiety about contracting the virus.

The virus-fearing passengers were hesitant to fly. Nonetheless, they were captivated by the prospect of flying with their pets. They decided to investigate the difficulty of obtaining letters attesting to the need to travel with ESAs.

Some virus-fearing passengers procured ESA letters from the medical or psychological professionals in their communities. Others found a simpler way to get them.

The virus-fearing passengers discovered that scores of professionals were willing to provide ESA letters. They could even obtain them online. They only had to fill out a form that listed a compelling reason to take their pets with them.

The virus-fearing passengers paid fees to the professionals who supplied the ESA letters. They were pleasantly surprised when the fees turned out to be $200 or less.

All of the passengers who intended to bring ESAs on flights brought their justification letters with them. Many brought additional items: distinctive ESA vests, ESA collars, ESA leashes, ESA medallions, ESA badges, and ESA tags. They hoped that animals outfitted with these displays of authenticity would not be questioned by TSA agents, fellow passengers, or Delta staff members.

CHAPTER 4

Skeptics

The Delta executives were delighted by the enthusiasm that some passengers displayed toward their ESA policy. They hoped that this enthusiasm would have a positive effect on their business. However, they soon realized that some passengers were skeptical of the new policy.

The skeptical passengers predicted that many passengers would be less healthy on flights with ESAs. They explained that those who were allergic to dogs or those who had a psychological fear of them would suffer.

The skeptical passengers also doubted that the ESAs would be as safe as service dogs. They noted that the ESAs had not received the hundreds of hours of training that the service dogs had received. They predicted that they would become disconcerted and then attack passengers, flight attendants, or other animals.

The skeptical passengers wanted Delta to return to a policy that allowed passengers to bring only fully trained and certified service animals on planes. They threatened to eliminate Delta from their future travel plans if the company did not comply.

Dellta executives were distraught at the responses of skeptical passengers to the new policy. Nonetheless, they still needed to hear from their flight attendants, who would be responsible for implementing the policy.

Flight attendants predicted that the presence of ESAs on planes would make it difficult for them to discharge their essential duties. They reported that even highly trained service dogs had attacked them, menaced passengers, defecated in the aisles, and barked uncontrollably. They doubted that the ESAs would behave better.

The executives were disappointed by the skeptical passengers and flight attendants. Nonetheless, they transmitted their concerns to USDOT. They pledged to follow whatever rules this agency established for ESAs on planes.

Easing Student Anxiety in Restrooms

The educational administrators in the Chicago schools had complex academic responsibilities. They had to manage teachers, discipline students, review curricula, conduct assessments, and monitor instruction.

The educational administrators had additional nonacademic responsibilities. They had to supervise school lunchrooms, provide student transportation, communicate with parents, and arrange interscholastic sports.

The administrators had to look after the indoor and outdoor spaces that were required for academic and nonacademic school activities. They had to ensure that the spaces were accessible, suitable, and safe.

The administrators developed policies to guide the use of indoor rooms and outdoor spaces. They hoped that these policies would be straightforward and easy to follow.

The administrators did not underestimate the importance of restrooms. They made sure that they were available to students, faculty, and staff. Historically, administrators had designated some restrooms for females, some for males, and some for persons with physical disabilities.

The administrators expected principals at individual schools to manage the restrooms on their campuses. They allowed them to develop the policies that made sense for their situations. They rarely reviewed these policies. They assumed that some of them had been in effect for decades.

The administrators eventually began to hear complaints about school restroom policies. They realized that they had to devote more attention to them.

Parents had been making many of the complaints. They did not believe that the restrooms were accessible to all students. They gave examples to underscore this point.

Some dissatisfied parents had children with disabilities. They noted that restrooms had been adapted for students with some disabilities but that they still were unsuitable for those students who had low vision or who were blind. They made the same point about restrooms for students who depended on service dogs.

Some dissatisfied parents focused on female students. They noted that their daughters used facilities that only had stalls while male students used facilities that had both stalls and urinals. They contended that their daughters did not have restroom access that was comparable to that of the males.

Some dissatisfied parents focused on transgender students. They noted that their transgender sons had difficulty using male restrooms. They explained that they had been insulted, threatened, and even assaulted. They insisted that they were not being treated the same as other males.

Parents with transgender daughters also were dissatisfied with the current policies. They explained that their daughters had been insulted by the other students when they had entered female restrooms. They noted that some of these incidents had taken place in the hallways as they entered female restrooms and some had occurred inside of the restrooms.

The administrators felt the pressure from the dissatisfied parents. They also felt pressure from personnel in the Office of Civil Rights (OCR) at the U.S. Department of Education.

The OCR staff had stated that Title IX gave them the authority to review the Chicago schools' restroom policies. They wished to make sure that those policies protected the interests of female students. They clarified that they would determine how the policies affected biologically born females, transgender females, and individuals who were questioning whether they would become transgender.

The administrators had attempted to be responsive to local parents and to the OCR staff. They had acknowledged that restroom equity was a genuine issue. They had been attempting to improve it. They gave examples of problems and the steps that they had taken to solve them.

The administrators admitted that female students had to wait unreasonably long periods to use school restrooms. They had been addressing this problem by adding more restrooms for females. They were making sure that the new restrooms could accommodate more stalls than the current ones. However, they had been able to take these steps only when they were constructing new schools or remodeling old ones.

The administrators also acknowledged the restroom problems that transgender students faced in their schools. In 2015, they had directed the school principals to assist these students with restroom access.

However, they had allowed the principals at individual schools to decide precisely how they would provide assistance.

The administrators hoped that parents and the staff at OCR would be impressed by the adaptations that they had made to their restroom policies. They waited to see their reactions.

The administrators were disappointed after they saw the reactions. They realized that neither the parents nor the OCR staff were satisfied. They therefore made another adaptation. They were confident that their latest adaptation would please everyone.

The administrators decided to make all restroom facilities available to all students. They could have referred to these newly designated facilities as unisex restrooms, gender inclusive restrooms, mixed sex restrooms, or all-gender restrooms. They found supporters for all of these terms. In the end, they decided to refer to them as gender-neutral restrooms.

The administrators made the announcement about their new gender-neutral restroom policy in 2021. They were eager to see how people would respond.

Enthusiasts

The Chicago educational administrators had assumed that the OCR staff would applaud their 2021 school restroom policy. They sent it to them and waited for their response.

The staff at OCR carefully reviewed the Chicago Public Schools' new restroom policy. They supported the changes.

Some parents had a special concern about restroom equity for female students. They believed that gender-neutral restrooms would address this issue. They supported the transition to them.

Some parents had special concerns about restroom equity for transgender students. They noted that these students were uncomfortable or mistreated in the current school restrooms. They believed that gender-neutral restrooms would address this issue. They supported the transition to them.

Some students were enthusiastic about gender-neutral restrooms and anticipated that they would feel safe and comfortable using them.

Chapter 4

Skeptics

The educational administrators had anticipated that the Chicago schools' revised restroom policy would be popular. They were delighted by the enthusiasm that some parents displayed toward it.

Not all of the parents were enthusiastic about the policy. Some were skeptical. They explained that they were more concerned about violence, racism, and bullying in the schools. They asked the administrators why they were focusing on restroom access rather than these high-priority problems.

Some of the skeptical parents did have genuine concerns about restroom equity. However, they worried that gender-neutral restrooms would have inadvertent negative consequences. They predicted that female students who used the new restrooms could be in grave danger from male classmates.

The skeptical parents predicted that transgender students could also be in danger when they used gender-neutral restrooms. They preferred the previous policy in which individual principals had met with transgender students and their parents to devise the best way to prevent physical and emotional abuse.

Some students were not enthusiastic about gender-neutral restrooms. They stated that they would feel uncomfortable and vulnerable in them. They added that they would try to avoid them.

RESPONDING TO QUESTIONS ABOUT CONTROVERSIAL EMOTIONAL SUPPORTS

This section focuses on the preceding two cases. The first case concerned the executives at Delta Airlines.

The executives initially had restricted nearly all pets from traveling in the cabins of Delta flights. They believed that this policy had the support of passengers.

The executives were distressed during the COVID-19 pandemic. They noted that people were flying less out of concern that they would catch the virus.

The executives collaborated with marketers and devised a plan to lure wary flyers. They would relax their animals-on-flights restrictions and welcome passengers with emotional support animals.

The executives assumed that their plan would be highly popular. They were surprised when it created controversy.

While the first case study centered on the executives at Delta Airlines, the next one centered on educational administrators in the Chicago Public Schools. These administrators developed, implemented, and monitored multiple policies, including those pertaining to restrooms.

The administrators historically had required that schools post signs identifying restrooms that were exclusively for boys and others that were exclusively for girls. They then restricted restroom use to students who had the biological sex corresponding to these signs. They assumed that students and parents supported this policy.

Some people did not support the schools' traditional restroom policy. They contended that it marginalized female students. They added that it was especially discomforting for transgender students.

Chicago's educational administrators decided to change their restroom policy. They began by replacing the signs on restrooms. They ensured that the new signs indicated that the restrooms were available to girls and boys.

The educational administrators assumed that their new restroom policy would be greeted warmly. They were surprised when it created controversy.

The following questions will assist you if you are going through this book on your own. They provide opportunities like those you would have in a college class where the professor uses the case method and help if you are in an actual class using this approach.

Question 1: Why Had Executives Historically Restricted Animals from the Passenger Cabins of Delta Flights?

The executives at Delta Airlines historically had allowed few animals into the cabins of flights. They worried about the discomfort that animals could cause most passengers.

How did groups respond to airline executives' policy? Focus on two groups: passengers and flight attendants.

Did the passengers have low confidence, moderate confidence, or high confidence in the airline executives' policy? How did the flight attendants feel? Explain the basis for your answers.

When answering these questions, as well as those that follow, you can rely on the information in this chapter. You might also use on some of the sources that are identified in the references at the back of the book. If you are reading this chapter with a group, talk about the best way to answer the questions.

Question 2: Why Did the Delta Airline Executives Change Their Animals-on-Flights Policy?

The executives later allowed more animals into the passenger cabins of Delta flights. They explained that the animals provided the emotional support that many passengers needed during the COVID-19 pandemic.

How did groups respond to the airline executives' new policy? Focus on two groups: passengers and flight attendants.

Did the passengers have low confidence, moderate confidence, or high confidence in the airline executives' new policy? How did the flight attendants feel? Explain the basis for your answers.

Question 3: Why Had Chicago's Educational Administrators Historically Restricted Restroom Use?

Administrators in Chicago schools historically had barred students from using restrooms that were not designated for their biological gender. They worried about the discomfort that they could cause fellow students.

How did groups respond to the educational administrators' policy? Focus on two groups: students and parents.

Did the students have low confidence, moderate confidence, or high confidence in the educational administrators' policy? How did the parents feel? Explain the basis for your answers.

Question 4: Why Did Chicago's Educational Administrators Change Their Restroom Policy?

Administrators in the Chicago schools later advised students that they could use all restrooms. They explained that this freedom promoted restroom equity and ensured that vulnerable individuals would feel safe and comfortable.

How did groups respond to the educational administrators' new policy? Focus on two groups: students and parents.

Did the students have low confidence, moderate confidence, or high confidence in the educational administrators' new policy? How did the parents feel? Explain the basis for your answers.

Summary

Executives at Delta Airlines believed that COVID-19 restrictions were making passengers anxious. They tried to ease their anxiety by allowing them to bring emotional support animals with them. They were surprised by the complex consequences.

Educational administrators in Chicago believed that gender-specific restrooms were making students anxious. They tried to ease their anxiety by converting these restrooms into gender-neutral facilities. They were surprised by the complex consequences.

CHAPTER 5

Religious Policies and Marginalized Students

When we took school prayer [out of Florida's classrooms] . . . disciplinary cases went up.
—Florida State Representative Charles Van Zant, 2012

[A new Florida law ensures that] a student may express his or her religious beliefs in coursework, artwork, and other written and oral assignments.
—Journalist Lindsey Kilbride, 2017

[The 2017 law] creates a legal quagmire for Florida schools.
—Anti-Defamation League, 2017

[Florida needs a moment-of-silence law to help students with] meditation, relaxation, connection.
—Florida State Senator Jason Pizzo, 2021

Chapter 5

[Florida needs a moment-of-silence law to] provide each student the ability every day to reflect and be able to pray as they see fit.
—Florida Governor Ron DeSantis, 2021

[Florida now requires that] public-school principals . . . institute moments of silence.
—Journalist Ryan Dailey, 2022

Families are encouraged to discuss the moment of silence with their children and to make suggestions as to the best use of this time.
—Florida Superintendent Rocky Hanna, 2021

[Students who don't get involved in the moment of silence will be] ostracized for not participating.
—Florida State Senator Lori Berman, 2021

Mayoral candidates in New York City competed against each other. They were disappointed when none of them attracted enough votes to win their elections. They recommended a shift to ranked-choice voting.

Florida's legislators wanted students to pause and reflect during the busy school day. They were disappointed that they did not have this opportunity. They recommended mandatory moments of silence.

Fostering Voter Deliberation

New York City's residents recognized the enormous influence and prestige of their mayor. Many of them aspired to one day occupy this office. However, they realized that they would have to wage long, expensive, and emotionally draining campaigns to win the election.

New York City's voters were somewhat predictable. More than 75 percent of them were Democrats in 2021. As a result, they could predict that the candidate who won their party's primary election would probably win the general elections.

The Democratic candidates found it difficult to compete in primary mayoral elections. They explained that they had to exceed the 50 percent threshold for the votes that were cast. They found it hard to reach that mark because they typically had multiple competitors.

Thirteen candidates were running in the 2021 Democratic mayoral primary election. They were nervous because none of them had a sure chance of exceeding the 50 percent threshold for votes cast. They also were nervous because they had to deal with a new electoral system.

New York City had designated ranked-choice voting for the 2021 election. This system eliminated runoffs and replaced them with a complex method of casting votes, tabulating them, and then continually retabulating them until one of the participants exceeded the 50 percent mark.

Voters had been prepped for the new voting protocols. They had been instructed to select the candidate who was their first choice for mayor. However, they also had to select those candidates who were their second, third, fourth, and fifth choices.

The voting was only the first stage in the election. It was followed by the tabulation stage. The tabulation stage was handled by poll workers.

The poll workers calculated whether any candidate had more than 50 percent of the first-choice designations. If they detected a candidate with this profile, they declared that person the winner. If they did not, they moved on to the next round. In 2021, they did not have a winner after Round 1.

In Round 2 of the tabulation stage, the poll workers identified the candidate with the lowest number of first-place votes. They then eliminated that candidate from consideration. However, they first examined the ballots that this individual had received. They focused only on the second-choice designations on those ballots. They treated those second-choice designations as if they had been first-choice designations. They then distributed them respectively to the remaining candidates.

Chapter 5

The poll workers had calculated whether any candidate had surpassed the 50 percent minimum at the end of Round 2. They reported that they had detected this candidate. They had no reason to move on to Round 3.

Enthusiasts

Elected officials in New York City had championed ranked-choice voting. They had assured their constituents that it would be fair and efficient. They were eager to see their responses to it after the 2021 mayoral election.

The elected officials had reported that Eric Adams had been the candidate with the greatest number of first-place votes after Round 1. However, he had not exceeded the 50 percent threshold needed to win. Another candidate, Maya Wiley, came in second, trailing by more than 9 percent. Kathryn Garcia came in third.

The elected officials noted that the situation in 2021 would formerly have resulted in a runoff election between the top two candidates: Adams and Wiley. However, they instead moved on to Round 2 of the ranked-choice process.

After Round 2, Eric Adams remained in first place. In contrast, Wiley was no longer the second-place contender. She had been replaced by Garcia, who originally had been a distant third-place candidate. In fact, Garcia had not only emerged in second place, but she was trailing Adams by just one percent.

Supporters of ranked-choice voting noted that Adams had acquired enough first-place votes to win the primary election during Round 2. They underscored the money that was saved by avoiding a runoff election. They beamed with satisfaction.

The supporters had another reason for being enthusiastic about ranked-choice voting. They contended that it was an antidote for the cognitive biases on which voters had relied during previous elections.

Persons demonstrated cognitive biases when they resolved problems using mental shortcuts. For example, New Yorkers who had been treated rudely by Texans might inappositely conclude that all Texans were rude. Meanwhile, Texans who had been treated rudely by New Yorkers might draw a similarly inappropriate conclusion. Clearly, both groups should have been more deliberative before drawing their conclusions.

Some voters exhibited cognitive biases when they voted for a candidate exclusively on the basis of gender. Others exhibited them when they voted exclusively on the basis of religion, race, ethnicity, occupation, or wealth.

Supporters contended that the ranked-choice process encouraged voters to evaluate the character traits, background experiences, and acumen of multiple candidates. They assumed that the voters then would be less likely to rely on mental shortcuts.

Skeptics
Elected officials in New York City had embraced ranked-choice voting. They had predicted that voters also would embrace it. They were excited to hear their responses to it.

While some voters were enthusiastic about ranked-choice voting, many were skeptical.

The skeptics said that they had not fully understood the new voting technique. They inadvertently had failed to list five choices for each office on their ballot. They wondered if other voters had been confused, made the same error, and undermined the election.

Some voters were skeptical for a different reason. They had fully comprehended the new voting technique and then filled out their ballots with precision. Nonetheless, they were shocked by the election results. They had not anticipated that the third-place candidate could not only replace the second-place candidate but nearly become the first-place candidate.

The elected official who backed ranked-choice voting had predicted that it would be more efficient than majority voting. They hoped that poll workers would validate that prediction.

The poll workers did detect a benefit of ranked-choice voting: They did not have to arrange and staff a primary runoff election. Nonetheless, they had been unprepared for the voter confusion surrounding ranked-choice voting. They questioned whether this confusion had negated any benefits.

The poll workers had another reason for questioning the value of ranked-choice voting. They recalled that it had been touted as a technique to minimize cognitive bias among voters. However, poll workers suspected that voters had spent so much time contemplating the balloting technique that they had little time left to contemplate candidates.

Fostering Student Deliberation

Some Floridians dreamed of serving as state legislators. They fully realized that they first would have to endure long, expensive, and emotionally draining campaigns. Nonetheless, they were eager to get started with their campaigns.

The candidates carefully planned how to cultivate supportive groups. They wished to focus on the groups that would have a great impact on the elections and, invariably, they focused on parents.

The candidates tried to attract parents. They sent them mail, contacted them over the internet, and met them face-to-face. They promised to alleviate some of their worries if they were elected.

The parents relished opportunities to confer with the candidates. They told them that they were worried about problems at school. They hoped that those candidates who were elected would address those problems.

Parents identified the school problems they had in mind. They were convinced that the schools needed expert teachers to enrich their children's academic progress, social aptitude, emotional growth, and character development. They explained that they needed expert teachers for critical academic areas such as mathematics, science, and technology. They added that they also needed them for elective courses such as art, music, and physical education.

Parents lamented that some of their children attended school in run-down classrooms and buildings. They wanted their children to go to school in clean, comfortable, and safe facilities.

Some of the parents complained that their children did not have opportunities to profess religious and spiritual beliefs at school. They noted that the textbooks, which once had covered religious topics, now eschewed them. They added that graduation ceremonies, which had once begun with public prayers, now avoided them.

The candidates listened attentively to those parents who wanted them to hire additional teachers and improve school facilities. They realized that it would be difficult to locate the funds needed to appease them.

The candidates also listened attentively to those parents who had religious concerns. They were convinced that they could address their concerns without massive funding. They pledged to expand opportunities for their children to express religious sentiments at school. Some went further: They pledged to provide opportunities for them to pray at school.

The pro-prayer candidates attracted enthusiastic supporters. Many of them then won their elections, went to Tallahassee, and served as state representatives or state senators.

The representatives served two-year terms. The senators served four-year terms. Both groups realized that their pro-prayer constituents would hold them accountable for the pledges they had made.

The pro-prayer legislators were ready to expand religious opportunities at school. However, they discovered that judges had complicated their efforts.

The judges had barred almost all forms of prayer at school. They permitted it only when it had a demonstrably secular function.

The pro-prayer legislators were not cowed by the judges. They passed a bill in 2012 that allowed students to make inspirational statements at school. They stated that prayers were prime examples of inspirational statements. They were pleased when the governor signed their bill.

The pro-prayer legislators had the governor on their side. However, they also needed educational administrators. They depended on the administrators to implement the provisions of the 2012 law.

The pro-prayer legislators noted that many educational administrators served in districts with pro-prayer parents. They were optimistic that these administrators would join them. In fact, they noted that some of the administrators had been allowing students to pray at athletic events or organize public prayer circles on school grounds.

CHAPTER 5

Most educational administrators were cautious. They acknowledged the prayer practices at some schools. However, they also highlighted the legal commotion that these practices had created.

The cautious administrators were sure that anti-prayer parents would challenge them if they were to implement the 2012 law. They did not think that the legislators had given them the legal protection they would need to withstand those challenges. They therefore hesitated.

The legislators looked for another opportunity to please the pro-prayer parents. In 2017, they crafted a bill affirming that students had the right to express their religious convictions while speaking, writing, or creating art at school.

The legislators worried that anti-prayer parents would brand their bill as unconstitutional. They were correct to be worried. They fretted when these parents asked the Anti-Defamation League to come to their aid.

The members of the Anti-Defamation League staunchly supported the anti-prayer parents. They assured them that they would challenge the bill, should it become law, as unconstitutional.

The pro-prayer legislators kept an eye on how parents were reacting to their bill. They also kept an eye on educational administers, who would implement any prayer-at-school law. Pro-prayer legislators worried that educational administrators had become timid from the legal wrangling that had surrounded the earlier pro-prayer-at-school laws.

Although the legislators did enact a 2017 prayer-at-school law, they were disappointed by its limited impact. They therefore began to plan for a subsequent version. They wanted to make sure that the new version did not pose any legal risks for educational administrators.

The legislators were ready to introduce their new bill in 2021. They set a goal of implementing it in 2022. This time, they made no mention of prayer. They simply required all schools to schedule a moment of silence at the beginning of each school day.

The legislators did not ask the school administrators to assume any special responsibilities. They only required that they schedule the moment of silence. In fact, they prohibited them from giving students advice about how to use this time.

The legislators used circumspect language to describe the moment of silence. One of them stated that it would foster "meditation, relaxation, and connection" among students. Another characterized it as an opportunity for students to "stop and reflect."

The legislators were excited after their bill passed both houses. They forwarded it to Governor Ron DeSantis.

The governor signed the bill. He stated that it provided students with opportunities to reflect. However, he did acknowledge that it also provided them with opportunities to "pray as they see fit."

Enthusiasts

The Florida legislators had championed the moment of silence. They had hoped that it would appease the pro-prayer parents who had voted for them. They were eager to see their responses to it.

Some of their parents had fond reminiscences about an era during which students had prayed at school. They were disappointed that the new law did not provide these opportunities.

However, most pro-prayer parents had a positive reaction to the law. They had observed the turmoil surrounding Florida's 2012 and 2017 prayer-at-school laws. Although they might have preferred a bold and expansive prayer-at-school law, they still viewed the 2021 law as a major achievement. They were grateful to the legislators who had crafted it.

Skeptics

Some pro-prayer parents had been disappointed with the moment of silence law. They viewed it as insufficiently robust. However, anti-prayer parents were disappointed for a different reason. They viewed it as too intrusive.

The anti-prayer parents contended that children would suffer from the moment of silence law. They explained that they would be surrounded by peers who had prayerful demeanors. They feared that they would feel socially compelled to model them.

The anti-prayer parents did not believe that the moment of silence law was connected to meditation and reflection. They were sure that it had a religious connection. They accused the governor of underscoring this connection by signing the law at a Jewish community center.

The anti-prayer parents needed allies. They were aware that some educational administrators had never complied with the state's earlier prayer-at-school laws. They hoped that they would not comply with the new law.

Some educational administrators did sympathize with the anti-prayer parents. They acknowledge that they had ignored the earlier and poorly crafted prayer-at-school laws. However, they explained that they had no choice but to implement the new law because it appeared to be cleverly disguised as non-religious.

The anti-prayer parents were disappointed with the educational administrators. They planned to challenge the law in court. In the meantime, they contacted journalists and asked them to publicize their reasons for challenging it.

Responding to Questions about Cognitive Bias

This section focuses on the preceding two cases. The first case concerned residents of New York City.

New York City's residents traditionally used majority voting for mayoral elections. To win, candidates had to attract more than 50 percent of the votes. When no candidate surpassed 50 percent of the votes, there was a runoff.

The residents supported majority voting. They believed that mayoral candidates supported it as well.

However, some candidates did not support majority voting. They were particularly critical when it was used for primary elections. They noted that the individuals who had to compete in runoffs could become vituperative, damage each other's reputations, and harm their political parties.

The disgruntled candidates had an ingenious plan to avoid runoff elections. They wished to switch to ranked-choice voting—a complex process that required multistage tabulations of the votes that were cast. They were elated when voters approved the change.

The candidates who espoused ranked-choice voting contended that it reduced cognitive bias and eccentric election results. They assumed that it would be highly popular. They were surprised when it created confusion and controversy.

While the first case study centered on mayoral candidates in New York City, the next one centered on legislators in Florida. These legislators had the responsibility for multiple school policies, including those pertaining to public prayers.

The legislators had at one time permitted oral public prayers in schools. However, they had received complaints from disgruntled constituents. They therefore permitted silent prayers instead. They hoped that this shift would satisfy the disgruntled constituents.

The disgruntled constituents were not placated. They told their legislators that they did not support oral or silent school prayer. They explained that both types of prayer marginalized students who did not profess any religion or who simply wished to avoid praying at school.

The legislators had changed their school prayer policy to accommodate silent prayer. They were ready to change it again. This time, they were going to fashion a policy that referred to a daily moment of silence rather than prayer.

The legislators passed a bill mandating a daily moment of silence in every public school. They conceded that some students might use the moment of silence to pray. However, they believed that others would use it to reflect on nonreligious topics. They were excited when the governor signed their bill and made it into law.

The legislators assumed that the new law would reduce classroom misbehavior, cognitive bias, and disrespect for religion. They assumed that it would be greeted warmly. They were surprised when it created confusion and controversy.

The following questions will assist you if you are going through this book on your own. They provide opportunities like those you would have in a college class where the professor uses the case method and help if you are in an actual class using this approach.

Chapter 5

Question 1: Why Had Mayoral Candidates in New York City Historically Recommended Majority Voting for Elections?

Mayoral candidates in New York City had at one time recommended majority voting for elections. They contended that it was superior to alternative voting systems, which increased cognitive bias, confused voters, and led to eccentric results.

How did groups respond to the candidates' recommendation? Focus on two groups: poll workers and voters.

Did the poll workers have low confidence, moderate confidence, or high confidence in the candidates' recommendation? How did voters feel? Explain the basis for your answers.

When answering these questions, as well as those that follow, you can rely on the information in this chapter. You might also use some of the sources that are identified in the references at the back of the book. If you are reading this chapter with a group, talk about the best way to answer the questions.

Question 2: Why Did Mayoral Candidates in New York City Switch Their Recommendation to Ranked-Choice Voting for Elections?

Mayoral candidates in New York City switched their recommendation to ranked-choice voting for elections, which they contended was more efficient than majority voting. They also contended that it would lead to less vituperative primary campaigns.

How did groups respond to the candidates' new recommendation? Focus on two groups: poll workers and voters.

Did the poll workers have low confidence, moderate confidence, or high confidence in the candidates' new recommendation? How did voters feel? Explain the basis for your answers.

Question 3: Why Had Legislators in Florida Historically Recommended Prayer in Schools?

Legislators in Florida had at one time recommended that students have opportunities to pray in public schools. They contended that these opportunities reduced classroom misbehavior, cognitive bias, and disrespect for religion.

How did groups respond to the legislators' recommendation? Focus on two groups: school administrators and parents.

Did the school administrators have low confidence, moderate confidence, or high confidence in the legislators' recommendation? How did the parents feel? Explain the basis for your answers.

Question 4: Why Did Legislators in Florida Switch Their Recommendation to a Moment of Silence?

Legislators in Florida switched their recommendation to a mandatory moment of silence in public schools. They explained that this practice accommodated students who wished to pray as well as those who had no interest in praying. They also believed that it could withstand legal challenges better than earlier school prayer laws.

How did groups respond to the legislators' new recommendation? Focus on two groups: school administrators and parents.

Did the school administrators have low confidence, moderate confidence, or high confidence in the legislators' new recommendation? How did the parents feel? Explain the basis for your answers.

Summary

Mayoral candidates in New York City competed against each other to win majority-voting-based elections. They were disappointed when none of them attracted the minimum number of votes needed for an outright win. They recommended a shift to ranked-choice voting.

Florida's legislators wanted students to pause and reflect during the busy school day. They were disappointed when they did not have this opportunity. They recommended mandatory moments of silence.

CHAPTER 6

Homeless Policies and Marginalized Students

In 2015, Los Angeles [Mayor Garcetti] declared a state of emergency on homelessness.
  —Homeless Crisis Architects Sofia Borges and
                  R. Scott Mitchell, 2018

[The homelessness in Los Angeles is] caused by trauma . . . insufficient housing and . . . things that have conspired from Washington.
  —Los Angeles Mayor Eric Garcetti, 2019

No [Los Angeles] policy issue is more pressing than . . . homelessness.
  —Committee for Greater LA, 2022

Individuals with mental illness, some of them absolutely unclothed, [have been] shouting profanities [from the homeless encampments by] elementary schools.
  —Los Angeles Superintendent Alberto Carvalho, 2022

Chapter 6

[The homeless encampment that is by my school creates] unsafe, unsanitary conditions.
—Unnamed Los Angeles School Principal, 2022

Mayor Eric Garcetti [has reversed his homeless policy and] signed legislation . . . criminalizing [some] homeless encampments.
—Journalist Natalie Shure, 2021

[The Los Angeles City Council reversed its policy by banning homeless] encampments within 500 feet of schools.
—City News Service, 2022

[The banning of homeless encampments near schools] is something to protect kids in our city.
—Los Angeles City Councilor Paul Koretz, 2022.

Mid-twentieth-century businesspersons placed ads on the *Lawrence Welk Show*. They believed that these ads would boost sales of their products. However, they were disappointed and switched their ads to other shows.

The mayor of Los Angeles constructed residences for the students and families in homeless encampments. He believed that the construction would boost his political standing. However, he was disappointed and switched his efforts to regulating homeless encampments.

Marketing Analytics

Lawrence Welk was a twentieth-century bandleader. He cultivated a regional audience during the 1940s, but he aspired to attract a larger audience.

Welk was invited to perform on national television in 1951. He eagerly grasped this opportunity.

Welk had intuition about the type of entertainment that viewers were craving. He directed his singers and instrumentalists to perform light and breezy musical numbers. He invited a live audience into the studio and gave them the chance to dance on camera during broadcasts.

Advertising executives represented corporations that were ready to sponsor successful programs. Advertisers assured corporations that Welk's show would endure for multiple seasons and encouraged them to advertise.

Enthusiasts

The advertising executives were pleased when their clients took their advice, funded Welk's show, and advertised their products on it. However, they still wished to carefully monitor the show's audience.

The advertising executives wanted to know the number of viewers who were watching Welk's show each week. They relied on companies such as Nielsen to provide estimates.

The Nielsen Company had identified a sample of households in which the occupants regularly watched television. They monitored which shows they selected. After compiling weekly results, they assigned high-viewership ratings to some shows and low-viewership ratings to others.

The advertising executives discovered that Welk's show had a high-viewership rating. They noted that it maintained this rating throughout the 1950s and the 1960s. As a result, they assured sponsors that they should continue purchasing ads on it.

The sponsors were pleased with Welk's show. The viewers who tuned it in were pleased as well. Week after week, the viewers never tired of the entertainment that it provided.

Skeptics

Advertising executives were on the lookout for groups with novel ways to compute television show ratings. During the 1960s, they learned about marketing analysts.

Marketing analysts wished to improve television ratings by factoring in the ages and incomes of viewers. They explained that this information was critical to sponsors because it revealed whether their ads were being viewed by people who could afford their products.

The advertising executives were intrigued by the marketing analysts. They were sure that they could provide useful information. They hired them to analyze Welk's show.

The advertising executives read the marketing analysis for Welk's show. They were not surprised to learn that the audience was large. However, they were surprised to discover that it comprised mostly seniors who did not have the discretionary income to purchase the products that were featured in their clients' ads.

The executives went back to their clients. They counseled them to switch their spending from Welk's show to one with a different audience. They suggested a show that had viewers who were young, who had ample discretionary income, and who regularly purchased products like those of the sponsors.

The advertising executives expected the sponsors to follow their advice. They were correct.

The advertising executives expected the performers on Welk's show to protest after they were cancelled. They again were correct.

The advertising executives expected the viewers of Welk's show to lament that they were losing a beloved television program. They were once again correct.

Educational Analytics

Eric Garcetti aspired to be the mayor of Los Angeles. He wanted to compete as a Democrat in the 2013 general election. However, he first had to win his party's primary election. He hired a team of political consultants to advise him.

Garcetti was initially impressed by his consultants because of the practical advice they provided. He later was even more impressed after he followed their advice, won the Democratic primary election, and won the general election.

Garcetti was elated by his political victories. However, he realized that he would have to engage in a reelection campaign in just four years. He asked his consultants to help him prepare for it.

The consultants were ready to get to work. They knew that Garcetti had struggled during the 2013 primary election. In fact, they admitted that he would not have won if it had not been for the support of the United Teachers Los Angeles (UTLA). They were determined to retain that support.

The consultants looked for urban improvement projects that the mayor controlled and that were connected to the schools. They knew that Los Angeles had more homeless families than any city in California. They reasoned that it therefore had more homeless students. They urged the mayor to highlight the problems that these students were facing.

The consultants discovered that Garcetti was getting ready to build public housing units. They suggested that he designate some of these for students and families in the city's homeless encampments.

The mayor followed the consultants' advice. In fact, he declared a citywide state of emergency for homelessness. He promised to respond to it by providing homeless people with inexpensive residential units.

Enthusiasts

The political consultants hoped that the leaders of the UTLA would approve of the mayor's plan. They carefully observed their reaction to it. They were relieved when they indicated support.

The political consultants were pleased with the UTLA leaders' reaction. However, they wondered how other key groups were reacting.

The consultants paid particular attention to journalists. They realized that they had a great deal of influence on the public's attitudes. They hoped that they would approve of the mayor's plan.

The journalists continually highlighted the problems of students and families in homeless encampments. They had aired hundreds of hours of videos and written countless editorials. They stood solidly with their mayor.

The consultants considered the city's educational administrators to be another extremely influential group. They wondered how they were responding to the mayor's plan.

The educational administrators were familiar with the educational rights of homeless students. They had learned about them from the 1987

McKinney-Vento Homeless Assistance Act. They relied on this act to guide their efforts on behalf of these students.

The educational administrators had established a homeless student office and staffed it with more than a dozen professionals. They expected these professionals to distribute educational supplies to students and their families. They also expected them to provide training to teachers, counselors, and psychologists at schools throughout the city.

The educational administrators were ready to provide even greater help to homeless students and their families. They came up with multiple suggestions. For example, some of them proposed to let them dine in school cafeterias, keep their vehicles overnight in school parking lots, and even take up residence in school buildings.

The educational administrators were ardent advocates for homeless people. They supported the mayor's plan to construct low-cost housing for them.

Skeptics
The mayor's political consultants knew that Garcetti was interested in how UTLA leaders, journalists, and educational administrators were responding to his homeless initiatives. However, they were sure that he also was interested in voters. They began to thoroughly investigate them.

The consultants already had confirmed that voters were concerned about homelessness. However, they knew that Garcetti expected them to apply campaign analytics to the voters.

Elected officials had learned about campaign analytics in a 1968 book, *The Selling of the President.* They discovered that the field of marketing analytics could be adapted for electoral politics. Since then, they had commissioned complex analyses of voters.

Garcetti's consultants hired analytics experts. They asked them to investigate how voters were viewing the plight of homeless families. They then shared their conclusions with the mayor.

The voters believed that homeless families needed help. They wanted city leaders to provide it. Nonetheless, some of them were skeptical of the mayor's plan to construct inexpensive residences.

The skeptical voters discovered that the mayor had spent $500,000 for each housing unit he constructed in 2021. They noted that he then had to increase that amount to more than $800,000 a year later. They gave him a low grade for financial planning.

The skeptical voters also investigated the size of LA's homeless population. They pointed out that it was expanding. They gave the mayor a low grade for political effectiveness.

The skeptical voters doubted that the mayor had fully comprehended all of the factors contributing to homelessness. They suggested that he turn his attention to drug addiction, mental disability, and psychological aberration.

The skeptical voters included parents. They worried about the danger that unregulated homeless encampments posed for schoolchildren. They called on city leaders to protect the schoolchildren.

Responding to Questions about Complex Spending

Two case studies were presented in this chapter. The first one concerned advertising executives.

In the early days of television, advertising executives were particularly impressed by the *Lawrence Welk Show*. They noted that it had an unusually large audience to view ads. They urged their clients to underwrite the show's expenses.

The advertising executives were pleased after their clients followed their recommendation. Nonetheless, they wondered how viewers were responding. They hired marketing analysts to find out.

The advertising executives read the reports from their marketing analysts. They were able to confirm that *The Lawrence Welk Show*'s audience was large. However, they discovered that it comprised mostly seniors. They doubted that the seniors had the discretionary income to purchase the products that were featured in ads. They therefore recommended that clients shift their financial backing from Welk's show to one with a younger audience.

Fans were annoyed when corporate sponsors withdrew their funding for this popular show. They were confused by their reasoning.

CHAPTER 6

The first case study concerned advertising executives. The second one involved political consultants who were attempting to help Mayor Eric Garcetti bolster his standing with Los Angeles voters. They assured him that the voters were extremely concerned about the city's homeless students and their families.

The consultants advised the mayor to fund inexpensive housing to replace the numerous homeless encampments throughout the city. They anticipated that he would win the support of many voters.

The consultants were pleased after the mayor took their advice. Nonetheless, they wondered how voters were reacting. They hired campaign analysts to find out.

The consultants read the reports from the campaign analysts, which confirmed that voters were genuinely concerned about students and families in homeless encampments. However, they discovered that the majority of voters wanted the mayor to do a better job of controlling the hazards that encampments posed to schoolchildren and recommended that the mayor shift his focus to regulating the encampments.

Some voters were annoyed when the mayor began to regulate homeless encampments. They were confused by his reasoning.

The following questions will assist you if you are going through this book on your own. They provide opportunities like those you would have in a college class where the professor uses the case method and help if you are in an actual class using this approach.

Question 1: Why Did Advertising Executives Recommend that Their Clients Purchase Ads for the Lawrence Welk Show?

Advertising executives recommended that their business clients purchase ads for the *Lawrence Welk Show*. They assured them that their ads would be viewed by this show's large audience.

How did groups respond to the advertising executives' recommendation? Focus on two groups: business clients and the show's television viewers.

Did the business clients have low confidence, moderate confidence, or high confidence in the executives' recommendation? How did viewers feel? Explain the basis for your answers.

When answering these questions, as well as those that follow, you can rely on the information in this chapter. You might also use on some of the sources that are identified in the references at the back of the book. If you are reading this chapter with a group, talk about the best way to answer the questions.

Question 2: Why Did Advertising Executives Change Their Recommendation to Clients?

Advertising executives applied marketing analytics to the *Lawrence Welk Show*'s audience and discovered that it comprised seniors who were unlikely to purchase their clients' products. They therefore changed their original recommendation and suggested that they purchase ads on other shows.

How did groups respond to the advertising executives' new recommendation? Focus on two groups: business clients and the show's television viewers.

Did the business clients have low confidence, moderate confidence, or high confidence in the executives' new recommendation? How did viewers feel? Explain the basis for your answers.

Question 3: Why Did Political Consultants Recommend that the LA Mayor Fund Housing for Homeless Students and Their Families?

Political consultants recommended that the LA Mayor construct housing for homeless students and their families. They assured him that he would win approval from the many voters who cared about homelessness.

How did groups respond to the political consultants' recommendation? Focus on two LA groups: educational leaders and voters.

Did the educational leaders have low confidence, moderate confidence, or high confidence in the consultants' recommendation? How did the voters feel? Explain the basis for your answers.

Question 4: Why Did Political Consultants Change Their Recommendation to the Mayor?

Political consultants applied campaign analytics to the LA voters. They discovered that the majority wanted the mayor to reduce the hazards homeless encampments posed for schoolchildren. They therefore changed their original recommendation and suggested that he focus on regulating homeless encampments.

How did groups respond to the political consultants' new recommendation? Focus on two LA groups: educational leaders and voters.

Did the educational leaders have low confidence, moderate confidence, or high confidence in the consultants' new recommendation? How did the voters feel? Explain the basis for your answers.

Summary

Businesses placed ads on *The Lawrence Welk Show*. However, they were disappointed by their limited impact on sales. They therefore switched their ads to other shows.

The mayor of Los Angeles constructed residences for the students and families in homeless encampments. However, he was disappointed by their limited impact on his voter approval ratings. He therefore switched his efforts to regulating homeless encampments.

Chapter 7

LGBTQ Disclosure Policies and Marginalized Students

[Students in St. Johns County, Florida are] choosing someone at school [instead of their parents] . . . to have [confidential LGBTQ] conversations.
—PFLAG Member Cindy Hill-Nobles, 2022.

[My daughter was bullied after the St. Johns County Schools counselor called her] by a fictitious male name and male pronouns in front of the other students.
—Parent Wendell Perez, 2022

[A classmate in the St. Johns County Schools] started yelling at [my daughter], "You're gay. You have no rights."
—Anonymous Parent, 2021

[This district will continue to] use the name and gender pronoun [requested by] the student [but it now will do so] with knowledge of the parent.
—St. Johns County Schools, 2021

Chapter 7

If the purpose [of the St. Johns County Schools' modified LGBTQ disclosure policy] is to protect children . . . it very possibly will have the opposite result.
—Attorney Jimmy Midyette, 2022

[The St. Johns County Schools] district is going to require [teachers] to effectively out [LGBTQ students] to their family.
—Anonymous Teacher, 2022

A filmmaker incorporated voice-cloning technology into his documentary. He seemed surprised after viewers found out and protested.

Educational administrators created an LGBTQ disclosure policy that excluded parents from learning about decisions that their children had made. They seemed surprised after the parents found out and protested.

Film Disclosures

Aging singers fretted as their voices deteriorated. They worried that they might have fewer opportunities to perform.

Audio engineers were ready to help the anxious singers. They had come up with ingenious software during the 1990s. They guaranteed that it would restore the melodic timbre and pitch that the singers once had exhibited.

The engineers referred to their software as Autotune. They noted that it could be used during studio recordings or live performances. They claimed that it transformed faulty vocal performances into perfect ones.

The engineers were excited when the artists agreed to experiment with Autotune. They were eager to hear their reactions to it.

The artists could not help but be impressed. Some of them publicly embraced the software. They candidly admitted that they were relying on it.

Some artists were embarrassed by the software. Although they used it, they tried to conceal it from fans, music critics, and journalists.

Journalists were on the alert for duplicitous singers. They focused on those who were aging, who still exhibited rarified vocal qualities, and who insisted that they were not using Autotune.

Journalists identified singers who had not been truthful about their reliance on Autotune. They gathered incriminating information and published exposés.

Journalists hoped that readers, listeners, and viewers would be engrossed by their exposés. They were disappointed when they showed little interest.

Journalists may have been disappointed, but they still were resolute. They continued to investigate cutting-edge vocal software. They eventually became interested in voice cloning.

The engineers who had developed voice cloning were extremely proud of their software. They showed how it could accurately reproduce the oral speech of any individual. They were delighted after journalists listened to demonstrations and then conceded that they could not distinguish individuals' artificial speech from their genuine speech.

Journalists were intrigued by voice cloning. At the same time, they were alarmed by it. They predicted that political groups would acquire it and then use it unethically.

Political groups did acquire voice cloning software. They then fabricated damaging messages in the voices of their adversaries. They broadcast these messages on television and posted them on the internet. They hoped that they would affect elections.

The journalists decried the fraudulent audio clips. They contrasted them with the audio clips that reputable filmmakers used in their documentaries. They noted that these filmmakers took great pride in the truthfulness of the information in their documentaries.

Morgan Neville was a filmmaker who was known for his professional integrity. He had been creating a documentary about Anthony Bourdain, a famous chef who committed suicide in 2018. He assured Bourdain's many fans that his documentary would be a candid, honest, and sensitive tribute to this beloved celebrity.

Neville intended his film to be truthful. However, he also intended it to be artistic, entertaining, and dramatic. He faced a dilemma when he was ready to use Bourdain's own words within key scenes. He located the words he had in mind. However, he was only able to locate them in print.

Neville could have designated an actor to recite Bourdain's words. However, he believed that the actor would diminish the dramatic impact of the words.

Neville directed his staff to search through the voluminous audio recordings that Bourdain had made. He wanted them to isolate words corresponding to those in the written statements. He anticipated that they could then extract those words and reassemble them in the order that they appeared in Bourdain's written statement.

Neville eventually abandoned the attempt to cut and paste an audio recording. He had a better idea. He could clone Bourdain's voice and be sure that the voice articulated the written passages with the intonation, pauses, and rhythm crafted to have the greatest artistic impact.

Enthusiasts

Journalists learned that Neville had used AI technology to clone Bourdain's voice. Some of them were not upset. They pointed out that Neville had used the technology to create a spoken version of Bourdain's own written words.

Many viewers agreed with the journalists who supported Neville. However, they noted that Neville acknowledged his use of voice cloning only after this subterfuge was leaked to the press. They admitted that his reputation for professionalism would have been more secure had he acknowledged the technology within the film's technical credits.

As for Neville, he was unapologetic. He admitted that he had used voice cloning and failed to disclose it. However, he bragged that he had deliberately moved outside the traditional boundary of documentary filmmaking. He compared himself to Bourdain, who he said had a reputation for "boundary-pushing."

Neville insisted that no one would have identified the cloned speech within his documentary had it not been for media leaks. He cavalierly urged viewers to enjoy his film and delegate any other concerns that they might have to a "documentary-ethics panel."

Skeptics

Some journalists were fine with Neville's use of voice cloning and his failure to disclose it. However, many were upset.

The skeptical journalists noted that Bourdain had maintained progressive political views. They assumed that he had disapproved of the voice-cloned videos that conservative groups had been airing. They were certain that he would have been horrified by Neville's use of this technology within a documentary.

Many viewers agreed with the skeptical journalists. They may have been initially mollified when Neville claimed that he had contacted Bourdain's family and obtained approval to use voice cloning. However, they changed their minds after Bourdain's widow denied that she had given approval.

STUDENT DISCLOSURES

Educational administrators in every state wanted their teachers to be effective and took steps to support them.

The educational administrators supplied teachers with academic resources. They provided comprehensive textbooks, current technology, comfortable learning facilities, state-approved curricula, and state-prescribed tests.

Administrators expected teachers to be alert for students with emotional or social problems. They told them that they should then refer these students to counselors, school psychologists, social workers, and medical professionals.

Administrators created district-wide policies to promote sensitivity, compassion, and respect. They made sure that these policies highlighted students who were marginalized or at-risk for being marginalized. When they gave examples of the students they had in mind, they invariably included students who were *Lesbian, Gay, Bisexual, Transgender*, or who were *Questioning* their gender identity (LGBTQ).

Educational administrators in Florida were dealing with the same issues as their colleagues in other states. As a result, they frequently duplicated their policies. They were impressed by a widely implemented policy that directed faculty and staff to address LGBTQ individuals by the pronouns that those individuals had designated.

The administrators in St. John's County, Florida, duplicated the prevalent policy on pronoun use. However, they added some additional provisions about disclosure.

The administrators assured their teachers and staff that they could disclose information to each other about students who wished to change their pronouns. However, they were not to disclose it to those students' parents. They explained that they wished to shield the students from unsympathetic parents.

Enthusiasts
The educational administrators did not broadcast their LGBTQ disclosure policy to parents. They realized that antagonistic parents could disrupt school meetings. They had observed the disruption that antagonistic parents had caused in Virginia's Loudoun County Public Schools. They did not want their local parents to replicate those behaviors.

St. John's County parents eventually found out about their district's LGBTQ policy. Many of them endorsed the practice of addressing students by the pronouns of their choice.

Some of the St. John's County parents also endorsed the practice of excluding parents from changed pronoun decisions. They worried that unsympathetic parents could cause children to become emotionally distraught, homeless, or even suicidal.

Skeptics
Educational administrators were pleased with the LGBTQ disclosure policy they had crafted for the St. John's County Schools. They were especially pleased after meeting with supportive parents. However, they became cautious after meeting with disgruntled parents.

The disgruntled parents wanted to know why they had been excluded from life-changing information about their own children. They were displeased when the administrators answered that they were trying to protect children from unsympathetic individuals, including parents.

The disgruntled parents questioned whether the administrators had fully considered the consequences of allowing students to change their pronouns. They gave examples of local students who had made these changes and then been socially rejected or publicly demeaned. One mother recounted that her daughter had tried to commit suicide because of the way she was treated by insensitive peers.

The disgruntled parents disapproved of the disclosure policy. They did not think that educational administrators had acted professionally when they created it. They asked them to reconsider it.

The administrators would not budge. They explained that they had acted professionally because they had created a disclosure policy that protected vulnerable students. They made it clear that they would stand by that policy.

The disgruntled parents contacted their state legislators. They asked the legislators to resolve this dispute.

The majority of legislators sympathized with the disgruntled parents. They drafted a bill that they entitled the "Parents' Bill of Rights." They explained that it prohibited schools from fashioning LGBTQ disclosure policies that excluded parents. They only needed the governor to sign it.

The legislators were pleased when the governor signed the bill. They promised to follow up by introducing additional parent-centered bills.

Posing Questions about Professional Behavior

Two case studies were presented in this chapter. The first one concerned a filmmaker.

The filmmaker had made a documentary about a famous chef who had committed suicide. He told the chef's numerous fans that he had selected previously unseen videos and previously unheard audio recordings. He assured them that he had been professional when making these selections and encouraged them to view his film.

The chef's admirers watched the film, and although they were pleased by some of the video clips, they had a different reaction to the audio clips. They asked if the audio was authentic.

The filmmaker responded candidly. He admitted that he had used voice-cloning technology to simulate the chef's voice.

Chapter 7

The fans were annoyed and told the filmmaker that he should have disclosed his use of voice cloning without being prodded. They questioned whether he had been professional.

The first case study concerned a filmmaker. The second one involved the educational administrators in a northeast Florida school district.

The educational administrators created policies to guide the manner in which teachers and staff members treated students. They stated that they had been professional when crafting these policies.

The administrators were concerned about LGBTQ students. They told their teachers and staff members to identify these students, listen to their concerns, counsel them, and give them advice. They added that they should address the students by the pronouns that the students designated.

The administrators noted that many school districts had policies for disclosing information about LGBTQ students. They therefore crafted a disclosure policy as well.

The administrators wished to be explicit about the groups to which teachers and staff members could disclose sensitive information about LGBTQ students. They encouraged them to share this information with each other.

The administrators also specified a group to which teachers and staff members should not disclose information about LGBTQ students. They forbade them from disclosing it to the students' parents. They worried that parents might respond inappropriately.

Some parents supported the disclosure policy. Others were disgruntled. The disgruntled parents asked why the policy circumvented parents.

The administrators acknowledged that they had purposely excluded parents. They explained that they had only been trying to protect the children from unsympathetic parents.

The disgruntled parents were disappointed with the administrators. They questioned whether they had been professional.

The following questions will assist you if you are going through this book on your own. They provide opportunities like those you would have in a college class where the professor uses the case method and help if you are in an actual class using this approach.

LGBTQ Disclosure Policies and Marginalized Students

Question 1: How Did a Filmmaker Characterize His Documentary?

A filmmaker made a documentary about a deceased celebrity chef. He insisted that he had been professional when making it.

How did groups respond to the filmmaker? Focus on two groups: journalists and viewers.

Did the journalists have low confidence, moderate confidence, or high confidence in the way that this filmmaker had behaved? How did viewers feel? Explain the basis for your answers.

When answering these questions, as well as those that follow, you can rely on the information in this chapter. You might also use some of the sources that are identified in the references at the back of the book. If you are reading this chapter with a group, talk about the best way to answer the questions.

Question 2: How Did the Filmmaker React to Criticism of His Documentary?

The filmmaker did not inform viewers that he had used controversial voice cloning. After disgruntled viewers questioned his professionalism, he explained that he had applied the technology only to passages that the chef had written.

How did groups respond to the filmmaker? Focus on two groups: journalists and viewers.

Did the journalists have low confidence, moderate confidence, or high confidence in the way that the filmmaker had behaved? How did viewers feel? Explain the basis for your answers.

Question 3: How Did Educational Administrators in a Florida School District Characterize Their LGBTQ Student Disclosure Policy?

The educational administrators in a Florida school district established a disclosure policy for students who wished to change the pronouns by which they were addressed at school. They insisted that they had been professional when creating the policy.

How did groups respond to the educational administrators? Focus on two groups: parents and state legislators.

CHAPTER 7

Did the parents have low confidence, moderate confidence, or high confidence in the way that the educational administrators had behaved? How did the state legislators feel? Explain the basis for your answers.

Question 4: How Did the Educational Administrators React to Criticism of Their LGBTQ Student Disclosure Policy?

The educational administrators did not inform parents that their disclosure policy had excluded them from learning whether their own children had changed the pronouns by which they were being addressed. Disgruntled parents questioned their professionalism, and administrators explained that they had acted to protect students from unsympathetic parents.

How did groups respond to the educational administrators? Focus on two groups: parents and state legislators.

Did the parents have low confidence, moderate confidence, or high confidence in the way that the educational administrators had behaved? How did the state legislators feel? Explain the basis for your answers.

SUMMARY

A filmmaker used controversial voice-cloning technology in a documentary without informing viewers. He insisted that he still had been professional because he had applied the technology to passages that the chef had written.

The administrators in a Florida school district created a disclosure policy for LGBTQ students who were changing the pronouns by which they were addressed. They specifically excluded parents from any information about the changes. However, they did not inform parents that they would be excluded. Administrators insisted that they had been professional because they had been attempting to shield students from unsympathetic parents.

CHAPTER 8

High-Priced Instruction and Marginalized Students

[Because] of the large numbers of children of limited English-speaking ability in the United States, Congress . . . [will] provide financial assistance [to the states for bilingual education]
—TITLE VII-BILINGUAL EDUCATION PROGRAMS, PUBLIC LAW 90–247, 1968

Bilingual education . . . was begun with the best of humanitarian intentions but has turned out to be terribly wrongheaded.
—FORMER BILINGUAL EDUCATION TEACHER ROSALIE PEDALINO PORTER, 1998

At no place in the day are [the students in my child's bilingual education classroom] learning to read and write in English.
—CALIFORNIA PARENT ALICE CALLAGHAN, 1996

Schools continue [to offer bilingual education because] they get federal funds for doing so.
— CONGRESSIONAL REPRESENTATIVE JEFF FLAKE, 2001

Chapter 8

Congress should triple annual ... funding for [school programs to help English learners].
—Century Foundation Fellow Conor Williams, 2021

College administrators encouraged students to take out loans for costly graduate programs. They assured them that they later would get the high-paying jobs needed to pay off their loans. They were surprised when the students did not get those jobs. They urged them to put pressure on the federal government to forgive their loans.

California legislators encouraged public school leaders to use federal funds to establish costly bilingual educational classrooms. They assured them that they would get enough funds to cover their costs. They were surprised when the school leaders did not get sufficient funds. They urged them to put pressure on the federal government for more money.

High-Priced College Instruction

College administrators had to make sure that their schools had enough funds to operate. Many of them relied heavily on the tuition from graduate students.

The administrators had to provide programs that would lure graduate students. They realized that some of these programs might not lead to financially rewarding jobs. They acknowledged that film studies, drama, and music had had bleak employment prospects for decades. Nonetheless, they still expected them to draw enough students to help pay for their cost.

The administrators also offered graduate programs that had robust job markets and that led to high-salaried careers. They cited engineering, analytics, accounting, and nursing as examples.

The administrators noted that hot-job-market programs were especially expensive to operate. They explained that they had to staff them with professors who could be making high salaries in their respective fields. They had to pay these professors competitive salaries to retain them on campus.

The administrators needed funds to sustain expensive graduate programs. They had been charging higher tuition for these programs. They insisted that they had no other option for covering their costs.

The administrators were not surprised when some potential students worried that they could not afford the high-tuition graduate programs. They tried to calm them. They told them that they could secure federal student loans to cover the tuition. In fact, they directed them to campus staff members to help them secure those loans.

The students secured loans for tens and sometimes hundreds of thousands of dollars. They were pleased that they could then afford their graduate programs. However, they were anxious about paying off their debt.

The administrators told the anxious students not to worry. They assured them they could easily pay off their loans after they had graduated and secured high-salaried jobs.

The students followed the administrators' advice. After they graduated, they were eager to obtain high-salaried jobs. However, many of them did not land them. They then realized that they would only be able to make interest payments on their loans. Moreover, they would be making those payments for decades.

The students went back to the college administrators. They reminded them that they had been lured into costly graduate programs with the assurance that they would secure high-salaried jobs. They told them that they had not secured those jobs, were not able to pay off their loans, and had become financially crippled.

The college administrators had a backup plan. They explained that elected officials had enacted federal loan forgiveness legislation for the graduates of for-profit colleges that had been poorly managed. They urged the students to create pressure on these officials to expand loan forgiveness to graduates from all colleges.

Enthusiasts
The college administrators had urged former graduate students to create pressure for loan forgiveness legislation. They kept their eyes on federal elected officials to see how they responded to this pressure.

Chapter 8

Federal elected officials had already been lobbied by college administrators. They had disappointed them after they had not expanded the loan forgiveness program. However, they were more receptive to this request when it came from indebted students.

Many of the officials told the students that they would support the expansion of loan forgiveness. They pledged to enact legislation.

President Biden became an ardent supporter of expanded loan forgiveness. He indicated that he would approve legislation after he received it from Congress. He added that he would expand loan forgiveness by executive action if Congress did not forward the legislation.

Skeptics

Students had taken out massive loans to pay for costly graduate programs. Some of them had family members or friends who had repaid their loans. Others worked for private companies or government agencies that repaid the loans of employees. Still others had secured the high-salaried jobs that they needed to make loan payments.

Graduates who were successfully paying off their loans tended to be skeptical about the need for loan forgiveness legislation. Those who had completely paid them off were even more skeptical.

Some federal elected officials showed little interest in loan forgiveness. They questioned whether this initiative would be too expensive for taxpayers to shoulder. They also questioned whether it would be fair to the many students who were paying off their loans or who had paid them off completely.

HIGH-PRICED SCHOOL INSTRUCTION

California's teachers worried about students who were not reaching their academic potential. Although they have displayed this concern for decades, they attracted national attention with the efforts they made during the 1960s.

California teachers had been looking for factors that would explain why students were struggling. They realized that many of them spoke *English* as their *second language* (ESL) or *had limited English speaking ability* (LESA). (They used the acronym LESA during the 1960s. They later replaced it with LEP, to represent students with *limited English proficiency*.)

California teachers had been instructing their ESL and LEP students in the same classrooms as *fluent English speakers* (FES). They noted that the ESL and LEP students were having difficulty learning English while they were trying to keep up with their FES peers.

Teachers observed that the majority of ESL and LEP students spoke Spanish. They had an idea about how to better meet their needs. They wished to separate them from their FES peers, assign them to Spanish-speaking teachers, and supply them with Spanish-language textbooks.

The teachers referred to the new classrooms as bilingual classrooms. They predicted that the students in them would flourish.

The teachers went to their administrators with their proposal. They hoped that they would approve.

The educational administrators were intrigued by the proposal. They anticipated that instruction in special Spanish-language classrooms would be effective. They also anticipated that it would be popular with parents.

The educational administrators did have a concern about the new classrooms. They noted that the Spanish-speaking students were to be segregated from their FES peers. They realized that this type of grouping would be politically contentious. They needed to get approval from their state legislators.

The administrators had another reason to meet with their state legislators. They needed additional educational funding to cover their expenses for specially trained teachers, special learning materials, and dedicated classrooms.

California state legislators met with educators in 1968. They wanted more details about the segregated bilingual classrooms. They were assured that the segregated classrooms were temporary measures and that the students in them eventually would join the FES students.

The legislators approved the educators' proposal. They then turned their attention to funding it. They computed the amount of money needed for special classrooms, teachers, and texts.

Chapter 8

The legislators realized that they would have to provide enormous funding to subsidize bilingual education. They doubted that they could come up with it. Nonetheless, they were still optimistic. They noted that the U.S. Congress had been working on a federal Bilingual Education Act (BEA).

The legislators were excited when the BEA was authorized later that year. They noted that it contained substantial funds for California's schools. They assumed that their financial problems would be solved and that their constituents would be pleased.

Enthusiasts

California legislators had stipulated that schools should establish special classrooms for bilingual learners. They were concerned about how parents were reacting.

Parents envisaged that the new classrooms would be staffed by skilled bilingual teachers. Some of them hoped that their own children would be taught by them. They were excited.

California legislators pointed out that the BEA of 1968 had made bilingual education less costly. They called this feature to the attention of educational administrators. They were interested in their reaction.

The educational administrators had been concerned about the cost of bilingual education. They viewed the federal government's participation as positive and were supportive.

The educational administrators were supportive for another reason. They had difficulty recruiting bilingual teachers. They noted that the BEA of 1968 directed funds to colleges and universities to prepare more bilingual teachers. They hoped to lure some of them to their schools.

Skeptics

After hearing from enthusiastic constituents, legislators were ready to expand bilingual education programs throughout California. However, they paused momentarily after they were challenged by some skeptical parents.

The skeptical parents did not wish to add more bilingual education classrooms. They were unhappy with the current ones.

The skeptical parents had informally compared students in the bilingual classrooms with students in English-language classrooms. They judged that the students in the bilingual classroom were lagging academically.

Some of the skeptical parents had children who had been assigned to bilingual classrooms. They provided personal observations about their experiences in those classrooms. They questioned whether their experiences were worthwhile.

The skeptical parents wished to remove their children from bilingual classrooms and place them in English-language classrooms. However, some of them had been blocked by educators who believed that their children would have difficulty acclimating to English-language classrooms.

The skeptical parents disagreed with the educators. They were not worried about their children acclimating to English-language classrooms. They anticipated that they would adapt readily, develop English proficiently, and achieve greater academic success.

The skeptical parents were upset when educators coerced their children into bilingual classrooms. They suspected that they were promoting these classrooms because of the federal funding connected to them.

The skeptical parents were frustrated. They had been disappointed by unsympathetic legislators and financially strapped educators. They were ready to take matters into their own hands.

The skeptical parents proposed a California state proposition in 1998. They explained that this proposition, which was assigned the number 227, would mandate that all students be grouped together in English-language classrooms. They began to gather popular support for it.

California's state legislators initially took little notice of Proposition 227. They were convinced that it would draw minimal popular support and have no impact.

The legislators eventually changed their minds. They were startled as more and more people came forward to express support for Proposition 227. They were shocked when the group became large enough to pass the initiative.

The legislators had wished to retain bilingual education programs. They predicted that Proposition 227 would have dire consequences. They implored voters to give individual school districts the authority for bilingual education. They eventually succeeded, but not for eighteen years.

Responding to Questions about Expensive Initiatives

Two case studies were presented in this chapter. The first one concerned college administrators.

College administrators tried to attract graduate students. They offered programs to enrich their understanding of subjects such as film, world languages, and art history. They also offered professional programs to prepare them for careers in fields such as veterinary medicine, dentistry, and law.

To fund graduate programs, the administrators depended heavily on tuition and continually raised it. They raised it most drastically for the high-salary professional programs that were staffed by in-demand professors.

The administrators anticipated that many graduate students would not be able to afford the tuition that they were charging. They encouraged them to take out federal student loans. They assured them that they could repay the loans with the earnings that they would receive after they later secured high-salaried jobs.

The students completed their programs and were ready to take jobs. However, some of them struggled to find suitable jobs. Even some who did find the jobs were not earning the salaries that they had envisaged.

Many students were unable to repay their loans. Some accused their college administrators of irresponsible financial practices and requested that federal elected officials intercede by enacting loan-forgiveness legislation.

The first case study concerned college administrators. The second one involved California legislators.

The California legislators knew that public school teachers expected their students to reach their full academic potential. They noted that they were extremely concerned about students who spoke English as a second language (ESL) or who had limited proficiency in English (LEP). They were intrigued when the teachers suggested bilingual education classrooms for these students.

The legislators encouraged the educators to provide bilingual education classrooms. However, they soon discovered that many of them struggled to pay for them. They told them not to worry. They explained that they would be eligible for special federal funds to offset their expenses. They were excited when those funds became available.

The legislators kept track of the parents who had children in bilingual education classrooms. They were gratified when many of them attested to the progress that their children were making.

However, legislators discovered that some parents were not satisfied with bilingual education classrooms. They listened to them complain about the limited progress that their children were making.

The disgruntled parents characterized the bilingual education classrooms as expensive and inefficient. They wished to curtail them.

Legislators had a ready response for the disgruntled parents. They noted that the bilingual education classrooms had not been fully implemented. They explained the federal government had not provided California with the money it would need for full implementation.

Legislators urged the disgruntled parents to create pressure on the federal government to provide full funding. They assured them that California's bilingual education classrooms would then become more effective.

The following questions will assist you if you are going through this book on your own. They provide opportunities like those you would have in a college class where the professor uses the case method and help if you are in an actual class using this approach.

Question 1: What Advice Did College Administrators Give to Students Who Could Not Pay for Expensive Graduate Programs?
College administrators enticed students into expensive graduate programs. They advised them to pay their tuition with federal loans. They argued that students would be able to repay the loans because their programs would lead to high-salaried jobs.

CHAPTER 8

How did groups respond to the college administrators' advice? Focus on two groups: federal elected officials and graduate students.

Did the federal elected officials have low confidence, moderate confidence, or high confidence in the college administrators' advice? How did the graduate students feel? Explain the basis for your answers.

When answering these questions, as well as those that follow, you can rely on the information in this chapter. You might also use some of the sources that are identified in the references at the back of the book. If you are reading this chapter with a group, talk about the best way to answer the questions.

Question 2: What Advice Did the College Administrators Give to Graduates Who Could Not Repay Student Loans?

Colleges observed that many of the students who had completed their graduate programs were struggling to pay off their loans. They advised them to put pressure on the federal government to forgive the loans.

How did groups respond to the college administrators' advice? Focus on two groups: federal elected officials and graduate students.

Did the federal elected officials have low confidence, moderate confidence, or high confidence in the college administrators' advice? How did the graduate students feel? Explain the basis for your answers.

Question 3: What Advice Did California's Legislators Give to School Administrators Who Could Not Pay for Expensive Bilingual Education Classrooms?

California legislators urged school administrators to provide expensive bilingual education classrooms. They advised them that they would receive federal funds to cover their costs.

How did groups respond to the legislators' advice? Focus on two groups: school administrators and parents.

Did the school administrators have low confidence, moderate confidence, or high confidence in the legislators' advice? How did the parents feel? Explain the basis for your answers.

Question 4: What Advice Did Legislators Give to Administrators Who Needed Additional Funds to Run Bilingual Education Classrooms?

California legislators observed that school administrators had received federal funds for bilingual education programs, but noted that many were still struggling to cover the costs. Legislators advised the administrators to put pressure on the federal government for additional funds.

How did groups respond to the legislators' advice? Focus on two groups: school administrators and parents.

Did the school administrators have low confidence, moderate confidence, or high confidence in the legislators' advice? How did the parents feel? Explain the basis for your answers.

Summary

College administrators advised students to enroll in expensive graduate programs. They assured them that they would get federal loans to cover the cost of their programs and then later get the high-salaried jobs needed to repay their loans. Surprised when the students did not get these jobs, administrators urged graduates to put pressure on the federal government for loan forgiveness.

California legislators advised school administrators to establish expensive bilingual education classrooms. They assured them that they would get enough federal funds to cover their costs. Surprised when the administrators did not get sufficient funds, legislators urged administrators to pressure the federal government for additional money.

Chapter 9

Disability Policies and Marginalized Students

The national discourse on school discipline has been dominated by . . . zero tolerance.
—American Psychological Association Zero Tolerance Task Force, 2008

Zero-tolerance policies must apply equally to all students regardless of . . . disability.
—State of Florida, 2022

Children have a constitutional right to an equal education, but . . . zero tolerance policies . . . make this nearly impossible for . . . students with disabilities.
—American Civil Liberties Union Florida, 2022

If your child [has a disability and] is confronted with a zero tolerance infraction: Know state and federal laws and school policies.
—Parent Blake Emmanuel, 2022

Chapter 9

If school officials are applying a zero tolerance policy to . . . students with disabilities . . . talk to an education lawyer.
—Legal Journalist E. A. Gjelten, 2019

Supermarket owners historically had not charged special fees to place new products on their shelves. However, they later worried about the financial risks they were taking and changed their policy.

Florida's legislators historically had allowed educators to collaborate with parents when students with disabilities brought weapons to school. However, they later worried about the safety risks that they were taking and changed their policy.

Supermarket Policies

Supermarket owners stocked their shelves with a wide assortment of food items. They hoped that bountiful inventories would entice shoppers.

The owners had to take risks when they chose items to stock. They had to decide whether to stock low-demand items such as unusual spices or products for people with special dietary restrictions. They realized that these items could sit on their shelves longer than others. However, they also realized that they could lure customers who would purchase these items as well as additional items.

The owners took another financial risk when they stocked perishable items. They realized that dairy products, fresh produce, meat, eggs, and fish had expiration dates. They expected to discard these items if they were unsold when their expiration dates had passed. They adjusted their prices to account for this waste.

The supermarket owners took still another risk when they stocked new food items. They had noted that more than 90 percent of the new items failed to consistently attract customers. Nonetheless, they hoped that their availability might lure some customers.

Supermarket owners historically had welcomed new items in their stores. However, they eventually were receiving requests from grocery industry representatives for more than thirty thousand new products each year. They judged that the financial risks were too high because they had to displace profitable items to make room for the new items.

The owners told the grocery industry representatives that they had changed their policy for new products. They explained that they would have to pay a shelf fee for each new item they wished to introduce.

The shelf fee might be as low as $20,000 per item at a regional group of supermarkets. However, it could increase to several hundred thousand dollars at a national chain.

The supermarket owners introduced shelf fees in the 1980s. They noted that airport managers and bookstore owners had introduced similar fees decades earlier.

Airport managers had a limited number of "slots" at which airlines could disembark passengers and board new ones. They had required the airlines to pay special slotting fees if they wished to use their gates.

Bookstore owners were in the same situation. They had limited shelf space for new books. They expected publishers to pay fees to stock a book and then additional fees to display it prominently.

Enthusiasts

Supermarket owners had confidence in shelf fees. They were sure that they would help their stores stay profitable. Nonetheless, they were anxious to see how food industry executives would react to them.

Some food industry executives were not surprised by the new fees. They understood the logic for imposing them.

The executives who managed large and wealthy food companies had the financial resources to pay the fees. They doubted that some of their competitors could. They anticipated that the resulting decrease in competition would work to their advantage.

Supermarket owners introduced new products in order to keep customers satisfied. They investigated how they were responding to their new fees.

Some customers selected the same products whenever they visited supermarkets. They rarely experimented with novel brands. They took no notice of the shelf fees.

Some customers learned about new products from promotional signs, printed ads, or videos. They were excited to try them. Although they may have been disappointed when they could not find them in local grocery stores, they continued to patronize those stores.

Skeptics

Executives at large food companies could afford to pay shelf fees. But executives at small and startup companies were in a different situation.

Executives at startup companies typically struggled to match the prices of established competitors. Moreover, they had not yet developed robust streams of revenue. As a result, they had little discretionary income for shelf fees. They were highly skeptical and decried shelf fees unfair. They claimed that such fees were designed to strengthen established companies but weaken fledgling competitors.

The skeptical executives tried to persuade the supermarket owners to eliminate shelf fees. When they could not, they appealed to the Federal Trade Commission and the U.S. Department of Justice. They were disappointed when these agencies did not take their side in the dispute.

Disability Policies

Florida's legislators had politically diverse constituents. Some of them represented voters who were predominantly progressive. Others represented voters who were predominantly conservative. Although both of these political groups were willing to pursue initiatives that did not have bipartisan support, they preferred ones that did have it.

The legislators met with progressive and conservative voters to discover important issues. They learned that the parents from both groups agreed that schools should be a top priority.

Parents wanted schools that were spacious and modern. They wanted them to be situated in their neighborhoods or close to them.

Parents wanted schools that were equipped with current technology. They also expected them to have appropriately equipped science labs, playgrounds, athletic facilities, band rooms, and cafeterias.

Parents wanted schools that were serviced by efficient and reliable transportation. They expected the transportation to bring students to their homes as well as to special events.

Parents set especially high standards for school personnel. They wanted high-powered administrators, caring teachers, and fully trained support staff.

The parents expected Florida's schools to maintain comprehensive operational policies. They expected these policies to address education, discipline, and counseling. They also expected them to be applicable to all students, including those with disabilities.

During the 1990s, parents added another item to their list of educational priorities. In fact, some of them placed it at the top spot. They explained that they had been terrified by people who had brought weapons to school and assaulted students and staff. They wanted schools to be safe.

Parents expected educational administrators to handle safety. However, they expected state legislators to get involved as well. They urged legislators to identify the steps that all administrators should take at their schools.

Florida's legislators would have been motivated to increase school safety because of the pressure from parents. However, they had another motivation. They were being pressured by the federal government to pass a statewide zero-tolerance policy.

Legislators explained that the federally sponsored zero-tolerance policy had several key provisions. It required that educators identify all students who brought weapons to school, report them to the police, and expel them for a year.

Legislators understood the logic behind the federal government's zero tolerance policy. They believed that it benefited everyone, including the students who were expelled.

Legislators enacted a zero-tolerance policy for the state of Florida. They made it clear that it applied to all students, including those with disabilities. They added that it applied to students with disabilities even if their behavior was the direct result of their disabilities.

Enthusiasts
Florida's legislators submitted their policy to the federal Department of Education. They hoped that this agency would approve.

CHAPTER 9

The federal agents had mandated that the states eliminate educator and parent discretion from cases in which students brought weapons to school. Nonetheless, they had not specified how they were to deal with cases where students misbehaved because of disabilities. They left this matter to the individual states. As a result, they approved the Florida policy.

Florida's legislators were pleased when they obtained federal approval for their zero-tolerance policy. They required that approval to receive federal educational funds. They desperately needed those funds.

Florida's legislators were still not sure how their constituents would react to the new policy. They paid special attention to the parents and hoped that they would approve.

Some parents were especially concerned about students with mental health disabilities. They believed that the risk they posed had been underestimated by soft-hearted administrators, teachers, and school psychologists. They heartily approved of the new policy.

Florida's legislators were pleased that some parents approved of their zero-tolerance policy. They anticipated that educators would join them.

Some educators had been threatened by students with disabilities. They believed that those students were likely to follow through on their threats. They supported the use of zero tolerance with them.

Skeptics
Legislators knew that parents of students with disabilities had been extremely pleased with the manner in which they historically had handled their children. They anticipated that they would not be as pleased with the new zero-tolerance policy.

Parents of children with disabilities were skeptical of zero tolerance. They believed that their children should be excluded from this policy when they misbehaved because of their disabilities. They argued that this protection had been guaranteed by federal legislation. They asked lawyers to back them up.

Lawyers throughout Florida agreed with the skeptical parents. They contended that the federal legislation affecting students with disabilities had precedence over the zero-tolerance policy. They encouraged parents to contest any disciplinary punishment that was dictated by the zero-tolerance policy.

Parents of children with disabilities had led the national drive for equal access to public education. However, they had recruited educators as allies during that campaign. They hoped that the educators would side with them again.

Many educators did take the side of the skeptical parents and their children. They provided testimonials about the negative impact that zero tolerance had on students with disabilities. They added that it had not made the schools any safer. They assured parents that they had the training to protect students with disabilities and their classmates from harm.

Responding to Questions about Controversial Policies

Two case studies were presented in this chapter. The first one concerned supermarket owners.

Supermarket owners had to make decisions about the food items that they would stock. They primarily selected products that were already popular with customers. However, they also selected some new products.

Supermarket owners made a stipulation with the food industry executives who lobbied for new products. Although they would place these products on their shelves, they would restock them only if they became popular. They explained that they did not want to clutter their shelves with products that were of little interest to consumers.

Supermarket owners had many requests to place new food items on their shelves. They eventually had more requests than they could accommodate. They had to decide whether they would remove some already popular items to make space for new ones.

Supermarket owners realized that they were taking financial risks with new food products. They wished to reduce those risks. They made a proposal to the food industry executives.

Store owners stipulated that the food industry executives would have to pay special fees in order to place new items on their shelves. They pledged to treat those new items differently if they began to sell well. They were eager to see how the food industry executives would react.

Chapter 9

Some executives were pleased. They represented established companies that could afford the shelf fees. However, executives from established companies correctly assumed that competitors who could not afford the fees would feel differently.

The store owners also observed customers to see how they would react to the fees.

Relatively few customers took notice that the stores had changed the way that they stocked their shelves. Those who did notice purchased hard-to-find items online or at different stores.

The first case study concerned grocery store owners. The second one involved Florida's legislators.

These legislators wished to be responsive to their constituents. They regularly contacted them to discover their concerns. They made sure to contact parents.

Florida parents had for decades made schools their highest priority. They told legislators that they wanted schools that were led by top-notch administrators, staffed by competent teachers, supplied with current textbooks, and equipped with advanced technology. They urged the legislators to take steps so that all children, including those with disabilities, would succeed at school.

During the 1990s, the parents raised another educational concern. They had been shocked by students who had brought arms to school and harmed peers, teachers, and staff. Parents urged legislators to implement statewide safety standards and monitor whether schools were meeting them.

Legislators were ready to get involved with school safety. They already were under pressure from the federal government to implement a statewide zero-tolerance policy. They explained that this policy would require schools to expel students with weapons and report them to the police.

Florida legislators had to decide how they would handle students with disabilities. They had a longstanding policy of collaborating with parents in all cases, including those where their children had been armed. They decided that they would replace this policy with zero tolerance.

Legislators wondered how Floridians were responding to their new disciplinary policy. They kept an eye on educators and parents.

Educators wished to keep themselves and their students safe. Some of them therefore supported zero tolerance for all students. However, others questioned whether it was the best strategy for students with disabilities. They noted that it would negate valuable opportunities to collaborate with parents.

The legislators were anxious about the educators. However, they were even more anxious about the parents. They wondered how they were responding to their new disciplinary policy.

Some parents supported the legislators. They conceded that zero tolerance was far from perfect. Nonetheless, they concluded that it was necessary.

Parents of students with disabilities did not think that zero tolerance was necessary. They wished to continue to collaborate with educators. They were annoyed at the legislators for changing their previous policy.

The following questions will assist you if you are going through this book on your own. They provide opportunities like those you would have in a college class where the professor uses the case method and help if you are in an actual class using this approach.

Question 1: Why Did Supermarket Owners Stock New Products without Charging Special Fees?

Supermarket owners experimentally placed new food items on their shelves. They did not charge any special fees. They believed that this policy was to their customers' advantage as well as their own.

How did groups respond to the supermarket owners' policy? Focus on two groups: customers and food industry executives.

Did the customers have low confidence, moderate confidence, or high confidence in the owners' policy? How did the food industry executives feel? Explain the basis for your answers.

When answering these questions, as well as those that follow, you can rely on the information in this chapter. You might also use some of the sources that are identified in the references at the back of the book.

CHAPTER 9

If you are reading this chapter with a group, talk about the best way to answer the questions.

Question 2: Why Did Supermarket Owners Start Charging Fees to Stock New Products?

The supermarket owners changed their policy for placing new food items on their shelves. They explained that they could no longer afford to take the financial risk of replacing popular food items with potentially less popular ones. They required that sponsoring companies pay special shelf fees.

How did groups respond to the supermarket owners' new policy? Focus on two groups: customers and food industry executives.

Did the customers have low confidence, moderate confidence, or high confidence in the owners' new policy? How did the food industry executives feel? Explain the basis for your answers.

Question 3: Why Had Florida Legislators Allowed Students with Disabilities to Remain in School after They Brought Weapons?

Florida's legislators historically had allowed some students with disabilities to remain in school even after they had brought weapons with them. They directed educators to collaborate with parents to make sure that these students did not harm themselves, fellow students, or the school staff. They noted that this policy complied with federal laws and pleased parents.

How did groups respond to the legislators' policy? Focus on two groups: parents and educators.

Did the parents have low confidence, moderate confidence, or high confidence in the legislators' policy? How did educators feel? Explain the basis for your answers.

Question 4: Why Did Florida's Legislators Switch to Zero Tolerance for Armed Students with Disabilities?

Florida's legislators changed their policy for students with disabilities who brought weapons to school. They explained that they could no longer afford to take the physical risk that these students posed to themselves, fellow students, and school staff. They directed educators to display zero tolerance for these students, report them to the police, and expel them.

How did groups respond to the legislators' new policy? Focus on two groups: parents and educators.

Did the parents have low confidence, moderate confidence, or high confidence in the legislators' new policy? How did educators feel? Explain the basis for your answers.

SUMMARY

Food industry executives historically had little trouble introducing new products into supermarkets. Some of them later became frustrated after they had to pay special fees.

Parents in Florida historically had little trouble collaborating with educators when children with disabilities brought weapons to school. They later became frustrated after they had to submit to zero-tolerance policies.

Chapter 10

Medical Policies and Marginalized Students

The push to reopen [Chicago's schools during the pandemic] is rooted in sexism, racism and misogyny.
—Chicago Teachers Union, 2021

Remote [Instruction] Saves Lives.
—Chicago Teachers Union Poster, 2022

The [Chicago Teachers Union's] complete and total shutdown of [face-to-face instruction] is just not fair.
—Parent Natasha Dunn, 2022

When you tell a parent that their kid can't be in school . . . that pisses them off.
—Chicago Pollster Brian Stryker, 2022

Chapter 10

[Face-to-face instruction is back in this city's schools because of] the parent activism, the parent voices, the parent demands.
—Chicago Mayor Lori Lightfoot, 2022

Professors gave students feedback about their academic progress. They contended that they made their feedback blunt so that it would be clear. However, they later tempered their feedback after they were accused of gaslighting.

Chicago's school chief gave parents feedback about COVID safety protocols. She contended that she made her feedback blunt so that it would be clear. However, she resigned after she was accused of gaslighting. Her successor then tempered his parental feedback.

Gaslighting at College

Professors set high academic standards for their students. They wanted them to excel. They prodded them with blunt remarks when they did not excel.

The professors viewed their blunt remarks as constructive criticism. They explained that they deliberately made them blunt to ensure that they were clear.

The professors were disappointed when their blunt remarks failed to motivate students. They acknowledged that they sometimes had the opposite effect: They caused students to become sullen, depressed, angry, or antagonistic.

The professors did not give up. They still intended to make critical remarks. However, they looked for softer language in which to couch their criticism. They hoped that that this type of language would reduce the chances of upsetting students.

The professors were even willing to repair the damage that they inadvertently had caused with blunt remarks. They resorted to stock phrases. They would state to a student that "You should not be so sensitive" or "You really need to act like a mature student with thicker skin" or "I have not said anything that justifies your behavior."

The professors were pleased with the tone they had taken. They assumed that the students would notice their change, detect their empathy, and cease their protests. They were surprised when students continued to protest.

The students believed that their professors were feigning concern for them. They explained that they were denying their own culpability and attributing all the blame to overly sensitive students. They referred to this psychological juxtaposition as *gaslighting*.

The students had learned about gaslighting in their psychology courses. They had discovered that the term was linked to a 1940s film about a couple in Victorian England. In that film, a malicious husband had artfully manipulated gaslights to make his spouse believe that she was insane.

The college students had a solution for gaslighting on their campuses. They demanded that colleges develop anti-gaslighting policies, post them on their websites, and ensure that professors followed them. They were surprised when the professors agreed with these steps.

Enthusiasts

Some students had been excelling in their classes. They had been receiving feedback from their professors about their progress. They were pleased with the positive tone of this feedback.

The students who excelled had never been subjected to harsh criticism. As a result, they had no reason to believe that they were the victims of gaslighting. Although they were only moderately concerned about anti-gaslighting policies, they viewed them as reasonable. They expressed their support for them.

Skeptics

Students who had been struggling academically had been subjected to harsh criticism. In response to that criticism, they had demanded anti-gaslighting policies.

The struggling students initially were pleased with the anti-gaslighting policies. However, they soon became skeptical of them.

The skeptical students realized that the anti-gaslighting policies had little impact on their professors. When they protested to their professors, they were told that they were being too sensitive. They immediately categorized this type of response as another instance of gaslighting.

Some of the professors became exasperated with the students. They contended that the students had been undermining their professors' confidence by making critical remarks about them.

The students had made critical remarks about professors in three ways. Some had made them face-to-face, others had relied on their colleges' evaluation-of-professor forms, and still others had used online blogs. They frequently had made their remarks blunt and demeaning.

The professors judged that the students were becoming more and more aggressive. They noted that they were especially aggressive when making anonymous comments. They stated that the students had become the true perpetrators of gaslighting.

Gaslighting in Public Schools

School leaders historically had concentrated a great deal of attention on students' academic well-being. However, they broadened their area of attention during the 2020–2021 COVID pandemic. They began paying as much attention, and sometimes more attention, to their physical well-being.

The school leaders wanted to implement policies that would protect students during the pandemic. They hoped to keep them physically healthy. They also hoped to keep them psychologically and emotionally healthy.

The school leaders had to assume unprecedented responsibilities during the pandemic. One of them stated that "we were . . . making public health and safety decisions," and this was "not something we've ever been trained for."

Janet Jackson was the CEO of the Chicago Public Schools during this period. She had to decide how the schools would handle health risks. She was eager to consult with important constituents, such as the leaders of the Chicago Teachers Union.

The union leaders shared Jackson's concern for the health of Chicago's students. They advised her they had a plan to keep them safe.

The union leaders wanted to cancel face-to-face instruction and instead teach online. They explained that the students could then isolate themselves safely in their homes.

Jackson took the advice of the union leaders. She announced her decision in blunt language. She stated that canceling face-to-face instruction would physically benefit students. She added that it also would benefit teachers, staff, students' families, and all the community members with whom the students came in contact.

Jackson noted that the teachers agreed with her decision and that the scientific and medical communities also agreed. She was pleased when many parents came forward and expressed support for her plan.

Although some parents did support Jackson's plan, others did not. The non-supportive parents had out-of-the-home jobs. They worried about finding someone to care for and supervise children who were isolated at home. They also worried about the academic, social, and emotional toll that would accompany isolation.

The non-supportive parents were angry with Jackson. They disapproved of her decision to cancel face-to-face instruction. However, they even disapproved of the tone that she had used when explaining that decision. They accused her of gaslighting parents to make them seem unreasonable.

Jackson did not wish to alienate parents. However, she also did not want to alienate teachers. She pleaded with the teachers to compromise.

Jackson could not persuade the teachers to compromise. She also could not persuade the parents. She did not conceal her disappointment. She resigned at the end of 2020–2021 academic year.

Pedro Martinez took over as CEO after Jackson. He announced that he intended to open the schools in the fall and resume face-to-face instruction.

The Chicago schools did reopen that fall. They then went back to a schedule that was comparable to their pre-pandemic one. As part of that schedule, they would close for a winter break in December and then reopen in January.

Chapter 10

Enthusiasts
Some parents had been disappointed with Jackson's pandemic protocols. They had had vocal confrontations with her.

The parents had anticipated additional health crises. They had demanded a voice in managing the schools during them. They repeated this demand to the new school chief, Pedro Martinez. They were pleased when he affirmed their role.

The parents expressed their gratitude to Martinez for pledging to listen to their advice. They interpreted his decision to resume face-to-face instruction as evidence that he was listening carefully.

Skeptics
The Chicago teachers resumed face-to-face instruction in the fall of 2021. However, they did not have confidence in this instruction. They saw too many risks. They had greater confidence in the online classes.

The teachers made it clear to Martinez that he had disappointed them. They accused him of partnering with parents at teachers' expense.

The teachers also accused Martinez of partnering with the city's mayor, Lori Lightfoot. They claimed that the two of them had been using gaslighting strategies to make teachers appear unreasonable and selfish.

The teachers looked for a way to demonstrate their disillusionment with the school chief and the mayor. They detected an opportunity after that fall's winter break. They announced that they intended to cancel all face-to-face classes, remain at home, and teach exclusively online.

RESPONDING TO QUESTIONS ABOUT PSYCHOLOGICAL MANIPULATION

Two case studies were presented in this chapter. The first one concerned professors who provided feedback to their students.

Professors regularly criticized their students' academic efforts. They contended that they made this criticism blunt to ensure that it was clear.

Some students disagreed. They believed that their professors were trying to undermine their confidence. They accused them of gaslighting them. They called for anti-gaslighting policies at their colleges.

The professors agreed to follow these policies. They then used softer language when they were making critical remarks. They assumed that they had appeased the students.

The students were still agitated. They accused the professors of perversely using the anti-gaslighting policies to demean them. They became even more agitated when the professors contended that their students were to blame for gaslighting professors.

While the first case in this chapter concerned college professors, the next one concerned public school leaders. It focused on the educational adaptations that they made during the COVID pandemic.

Janet Jackson was the CEO of the Chicago Public Schools during the 2020–2021 academic year. She realized that parents needed accurate information about the steps that the schools were taking to keep their children virus-free during a pandemic. She told them that she would close the schools, terminate face-to-face instruction, and substitute online instruction.

Jackson deliberately presented the parents with blunt information. She assumed that they would be grateful because the information would be clear.

Some parents were grateful to Jackson. Moreover, they agreed that she should close the schools.

Other parents were not grateful to the school chief. They accused her of using demeaning language to gaslight them for disagreeing with her plan. They called for her to resign.

Pedro Martinez became Chicago's school chief during the 2021–2022 academic year. He made sure to meet with parents about the best way to protect their children. He used softer language to affirm his willingness to cooperate with them.

Martinez was pleased when hardly any parents complained about gaslighting. However, he was distressed when his teachers contended that he was using this strategy on them.

The following questions will assist you if you are going through this book on your own. They provide opportunities like those you would have in a college class where the professor uses the case method and help if you are in an actual class using this approach.

Chapter 10

Question 1: Why Did Professors Make Blunt Remarks about Students' Academic Progress?

Professors made blunt remarks to students about their academic progress. They contended that they made them blunt to ensure that they were clear.

How did different groups respond to the professors' remarks? Focus on two groups: students who were excelling academically and students who were struggling academically.

Did the students who were excelling academically have low confidence, moderate confidence, or high confidence in the professors' remarks? How did the students who were struggling feel? Explain the basis for your answers.

When answering these questions, as well as those that follow, you can rely on the information in this chapter. You might also use some of the sources that are identified in the references at the back of the book. If you are reading this chapter with a group, talk about the best way to answer the questions.

Question 2: Why Did Professors Switch to Softer Remarks?

Professors made blunt remarks, and students accused them of gaslighting. So they switched to softer remarks in an effort to appease the students.

How did different groups respond to the professors' new remarks? Focus on two groups: students who were excelling academically and students who were struggling academically.

Did the students who were excelling academically have low confidence, moderate confidence, or high confidence in the professors' new remarks? How did the students who were struggling feel? Explain the basis for your answers.

Question 3: Why Did a Chicago School Chief Make Blunt Remarks about COVID Protocols?

Janet Jackson was the CEO of the Chicago Public Schools during the pandemic year of 2020–2021. She made blunt remarks to parents about COVID protocols. She contended that she made the remarks blunt to ensure that they were clear.

How did diverse groups respond to this school chief's remarks? Focus on two groups: parents who supported school closures and parents who opposed school closures.

Did the parents who supported school closures have low confidence, moderate confidence, or high confidence in this school chief's remarks? How did the parents who opposed school closures feel? Explain the basis for your answers.

Question 4: Why Did the Chicago School Chief's Successor Switch to Softer Remarks?

Pedro Martinez followed Jackson as the new CEO of the Chicago Public Schools. He was aware that his predecessor had made blunt remarks about COVID protocols and then faced accusations of gaslighting parents. He switched to softer remarks in an effort to appease parents.

How did diverse groups respond to this new school chief's remarks? Focus on two groups: parents who supported school closures and parents who opposed school closures.

Did the parents who supported school closures have low confidence, moderate confidence, or high confidence in this new school chief's remarks? How did the parents who opposed school closures feel? Explain the basis for your answers.

Summary

Professors gave students blunt but clear feedback about their academic progress. However, they tempered their feedback after they were accused of gaslighting.

The CEO of the Chicago Public Schools gave parents blunt but clear feedback about COVID safety protocols. However, she resigned after she was accused of gaslighting. Her successor then tempered his feedback.

Chapter 11

Military Service and Marginalized Students

Challenges of military service [affect] both active-duty and veteran service members.
      —Butler Center for Research, 2018

There are high rates of psychological disorders . . . among . . . service members' families.
      —U.S. Institute of Medicine, 2014

[Growing up in a military family, my siblings and I] supported our parents through 12 moves and two combat deployments.
      —Nora Anderson, 2021

My mom cried and I was pretty scared that my [combat-deployed] dad was going to die.
      —Unidentified Child, 2019

Chapter 11

Wartime parental deployments can be one of the most stressful events of a child's life.
—Mental Health Professionals Fianna Sogomonyan and Janice Cooper, 2010

Children of deployed military parents [are] more at risk for alcohol [and] drug use.
—Psychiatrist Stephan Arndt, 2022

Defense attorneys were convinced that troubled inner-city youths suffered from urban crime syndrome. They recommended that they be treated with therapeutic social programs.

Psychiatrists were convinced that troubled students who had military parents suffered from military family syndrome. They recommended that they be treated with therapeutic psychological programs.

Urban Crime Syndrome

Court-appointed defense attorneys frequently represented inner-city youths who were accused of crimes. They found their jobs extremely difficult when these youths had made confessions to police, been linked to crime-scene evidence, been identified by witnesses, or appeared in incriminating videos.

Challenged though the attorneys may have been, they resolved to represent the inner-city youths effectively. They employed the traditional legal strategies that they had learned in law school. For example, they disputed police procedures, witness accounts, crime-scene evidence, and crime-scene videos.

The attorneys who employed traditional legal strategies hoped to persuade judges to treat their clients leniently. They were disappointed when they failed.

The attorneys searched for more effective strategies. They examined the strategies that defense lawyers had used when they had to overcome enormous obstacles.

The attorneys began by reviewing cases in which spouses had confessed to killing their partners but then been found innocent at their trials. They noted that many of them had been portrayed as individuals who were trying to survive intolerable situations with abusive partners.

The lawyers who represented accused spouses contended that their clients suffered from *battered spouse syndrome*. They referred to the courtroom strategy they employed as the *battered spouse defense*.

The attorneys who represented inner-city youths contended that their clients suffered from a syndrome that was comparable to *battered spouse syndrome*. They argued that youths suffered from *urban crime syndrome*.

The attorneys stressed that their clients routinely had dealt with dangerous situations in inner-city neighborhoods. They believed that their involvement in those experiences should shield them from harsh punishments.

The attorneys also had advice about how to reduce the impact of urban crime syndrome. They recommended community-wide rehabilitation programs. However, they made it clear that these programs required collaboration from elected officials.

The attorneys identified the type of collaboration they had in mind. They expected elected officials to reduce the funding they were directing to police and corrections officers and redirect it to educators, mental health workers, and career training specialists.

Enthusiasts

The defense attorneys needed help to employ the urban crime defense successfully. They enlisted the accused youths.

The defense attorneys explained to the accused youths that they could help by the manner in which they responded to questions during their trials. They told them to highlight the impact that their neighborhoods had had on them. They were pleased when they followed their advice and made a positive impression on district attorneys, judges, and jurors.

The defense attorneys needed still more help to arrange a successful urban crime defense. They asked the parents of the accused youths to cooperate. They told them to testify about the troublesome neighborhoods in which they had raised their children.

The defense attorneys were not surprised that they had the support of inner-city youths and their parents. However, they hoped that they would receive broader support. They tried to recruit elected officials.

Some elected officials had championed social and educational programs for inner city youths. They characterized urban crime syndrome as a powerful rationale for initiating, maintaining, and expanding those programs. They were extremely supportive of the defense attorneys.

The defense attorneys also tried to recruit legal scholars. They noted that some of them had published books and reports about pervasive crime in inner-city neighborhoods. They were gratified when they expressed confidence in the reality of urban crime syndrome.

Some of the legal scholars went further to assist the defense attorneys. They appeared as expert witnesses during high-profile court cases. They also collaborated with journalists to make sophisticated legal arguments accessible to a wide audience.

Skeptics

Not all legal scholars supported the use of urban crime defense. The skeptical scholars did not doubt that the amount of crime in urban communities exceeded that in other communities. However, they questioned whether it was the result of urban crime syndrome.

The skeptical scholars also questioned whether a defense based on urban crime syndrome would be persuasive in courtrooms. They were aware that persons who admitted killing their partners had used the battered spouse defense successfully. However, they did not believe that youths who had been arrested for illegal activities could use the urban crime defense and be as credible.

The skeptical scholars pointed out that the defendants who used the battered spouse defense had been convincing because their lives were threatened. They asked whether the inner-city youths who used the urban crime defense would be able to make this contention.

MILITARY FAMILY SYNDROME

Members of the military could display unusual psychological symptoms. Some of them displayed them while they were in combat. Others displayed them after they returned from combat. They caught the attention of their superiors.

The military superiors referred the service members for psychological evaluations. They sent them to the medical personnel, mental health specialists, or military psychiatrists at their bases.

The service members were not the only ones who displayed unusual psychological symptoms. Members of their families, including their children, displayed them. Many of these children then misbehaved at school.

Teachers could not help but notice the misbehaving students. Some of these teachers worked at schools on military bases. Others taught at public schools in nearby communities.

The teachers had strategies for handling misbehaving students. Some verbally reprimanded them. Others relied on harsher punishments: They isolated them from their classmates, assigned them extra schoolwork, or prevented them from participating in clubs and sports.

The teachers kept records of the types of misbehavior that their students displayed. They noted that that some of those from military families were abusing alcohol, using drugs, brandishing weapons, or threatening peers. They were not prepared to handle the more serious cases on their own. They contacted the students' parents.

Military parents were understandably distressed when they learned that their children were misbehaving. Some of them wished to address these problems on their own. However, they did not always have this option.

The parents who had their children enrolled at military-based schools had to follow the protocols at those schools. When they were required to send their children to mental health clinics for evaluation, they frequently sent them to the closest military mental health clinic.

Don LaGrone was a psychiatrist who had a special concern for the young patients who were being sent to the military mental health clinics. During the 1970s, he carefully reviewed their records.

LaGrone noticed that some of the children had parents who were combat deployed. He speculated that they might be experiencing anxiety about the safety of their parents. He used the term *military family syndrome* to describe this form of anxiety. He suspected that it might be the reason that the students were misbehaving at school.

Enthusiasts

Military psychiatrists were intrigued by LaGrone's insight. They noted that some of the troubled youths with whom they had dealt had combat-deployed parents.

The military psychiatrists also noted that some of their young patients who were extremely anxious did not have combat-deployed parents. They wondered about the source of their anxiety.

The military psychiatrists listened as their young patients described the stress that they had felt as they had moved repeatedly from one community to the next, left friends behind, and abandoned comforting routines. They became convinced that their stress was just as debilitating as that of their peers with combat-deployed parents.

The psychiatrists were ready to help the troubled students. However, they needed assistance. They contacted the students' parents.

The parents felt enormous guilt. They worried that they might inadvertently have been responsible for their children's problems. They were eager to collaborate with the psychiatrists.

The parents felt better after the psychiatrists told them that their children were suffering from a disruptive psychological syndrome. They also felt better after the psychiatrists assured them that they could reduce the impact of this syndrome.

The psychiatrists described the steps that the parents take. They recommended that they scrutinize their children for signs of anxiety, alert mental health specialists when they detected them, and then refer their children to specialists for evaluation and treatment.

The military psychiatrists also asked educators to collaborate with them. They urged them to follow the advice that they had given to parents: look for signs of anxiety and then immediately refer their children for professional evaluation and treatment.

The military psychiatrists examined the youths who were sent to them. They tried to diagnose their problems and the sources of their problems. However, they also tried to help them deal with their problems.

The military psychiatrists had to devote enormous amounts of time to treating each student. They looked for less burdensome procedures. They searched for procedures that they could incorporate into a structured program. They hoped that they could then offer this program on every military base.

The *Exceptional Family Military Program* (EFMP) was established in the early 1980s. It was intended to help children who suffered from mental health problems, such as military family syndrome.

The parents were excited about the EFMP. They were eager to get help for their children with mental health problems. However, they hoped that military leaders would adapt it to help children with social, emotional, physical, and cognitive disabilities. They were pleased when the military leaders responded quickly to their request.

Parents, teachers, and mental health professionals participated in the EFMP. They were assisted by high-powered teams comprising physicians, counselors, nurses, speech-language pathologists, school psychologists, applied behavior analysts, physical therapists, and other specialists.

Skeptics

Some educators were not eager to refer students to be screened for military family syndrome. They had reservations about the syndrome and the treatments associated with it.

The skeptical educators doubted that psychological evaluations based on military family syndrome would benefit students. They also doubted that they would improve school discipline. They traditionally had punished misbehaving students. They wished to continue punishing all misbehaving students, including those with military parents.

Even some psychiatrists were reluctant to embrace military family syndrome. They dealt extensively with youths from military families. They had employed traditional, well-validated procedures with these students. They explained the procedures.

The skeptical psychiatrists met with the students who were referred to them. They exhaustively diagnosed them. After they had completed their diagnoses, they prescribed treatments. They then observed how the students were responding. They regularly modified the treatments to make them more effective.

The skeptical psychiatrists had confidence in their traditional diagnostic and therapeutic procedures. They were not ready to classify students as victims of military family syndrome. Nonetheless, they did concede that this shift would enable them to handle more patients.

Responding to Questions about Complex Behaviors

Two case studies were presented in this chapter. The first one concerned the attorneys who represented inner-city youths in court. These attorneys claimed that their defendants' behaviors could be attributed to urban crime syndrome.

The attorneys stated that their defendants had been influenced by the high-crime neighborhoods in which they lived. They argued that they should be treated leniently.

The attorneys also had advice about how to reduce the impact of urban crime syndrome. They recommended community-wide rehabilitation programs. However, they made it clear that these programs required collaboration. They envisaged collaboration among police officers, corrections officers, educators, mental healthcare workers, and career training specialists.

The attorneys even identified a way to pay for the collaborative services. They expected elected officials to reduce funding for the police and corrections officers and redirect it to the educators, mental healthcare workers, and career training specialists.

While the first case study in this chapter concerned defense attorneys, the next one focused on psychiatrists. The psychiatrists were concerned about troubled youths from military families.

The psychiatrists stated that these youths suffered from military family syndrome. They argued that they should be treated leniently when they misbehaved.

The psychiatrists had advice about how to reduce the impact of military family syndrome. They recommended mental health programs. However, they made it clear that these programs required the collaboration of many groups, including educators.

The psychiatrists explained how educators could refocus their efforts. They expected them to spend less time disciplining students and more time referring them for psychological evaluation.

The following questions will assist you if you are going through this book on your own. They provide opportunities like those you would have in a college class where the professor uses the case method and help if you are in an actual class using this approach.

Question 1: Why Did Attorneys Use Standard Legal Strategies to Defend Inner City Youths in Court?

Defense attorneys represented inner-city youths in court. They used standard legal strategies. For example, they challenged police procedures, witness accounts, and crime-scene evidence. They expected these strategies to shield misbehaving youths from harsh punishments.

How did different groups respond to the defense strategies that the attorneys were employing? Focus on two groups: parents and elected officials.

Did the parents have low confidence, moderate confidence, or high confidence in the defense strategies that the attorneys were employing? How did the elected officials feel? Explain the basis for your answers.

When answering these questions, as well as those that follow, you can rely on the information in this chapter. You might also use some of the sources that are identified in the references at the back of the book. If you are reading this chapter with a group, talk about the best way to answer the questions.

Question 2: Why Did Attorneys Turn to Urban Crime Defense?

Defense attorneys were disappointed when standard legal strategies failed to shield inner-city youths from harsh punishments in court. They therefore began to rely on Urban Crime Defense. After attributing the youths' crimes to their dangerous neighborhoods, they hoped that the youths would be treated less harshly.

How did different groups respond to the new defense strategy that the attorneys were employing? Focus on two groups: parents and elected officials.

Chapter 11

Did the parents have low confidence, moderate confidence, or high confidence in the new defense strategy that the attorneys were employing? How did the elected officials feel? Explain the basis for your answers.

Question 3: Why Did Psychiatrists Apply Standard Diagnostic Procedures to Youths from Military Families?

Psychiatrists examined youths from military families. They applied standard diagnostic procedures. As examples, they gathered data about unusual behaviors, posited causes for them, prescribed treatments, and then observed the impact of those treatments. They hoped that these procedures would shield misbehaving youths from harsh punishments at school.

How did different groups respond to the diagnostic procedures that the psychiatrists were employing? Focus on two groups: parents and educators.

Did the parents have low confidence, moderate confidence, or high confidence in the diagnostic procedures that the psychiatrists were employing? How did the educators feel? Explain the basis for your answers.

Question 4: Why Did Psychiatrists Turn to Military Family Syndrome?

Psychiatrists were disappointed when standard diagnostic procedures failed to shield military-family youths from harsh punishments at school. They therefore began to rely on military family syndrome. After attributing the youths' behaviors to their stressful home lives, they hoped that the youths would be treated less harshly.

How did different groups respond to the new diagnostic procedure that the psychiatrists were employing? Focus on two groups: parents and educators.

Did the parents have low confidence, moderate confidence, or high confidence in the new diagnostic procedure that the psychiatrists were employing? How did the educators feel? Explain the basis for your answers.

SUMMARY

Defense attorneys noted that a disproportionate number of inner-city youths were appearing in criminal courts. They were convinced that they suffered from urban crime syndrome. They believed that they should be spared from harsh punishments and participate in therapeutic social programs instead.

Psychiatrists noted that a disproportionate number of military-family youths were appearing at mental health clinics. They were convinced that they suffered from military family syndrome. They believed that they should be spared from harsh punishments and participate in therapeutic psychological programs instead.

CHAPTER 12

Immigration Status and Marginalized Students

Migrant encounters [have] more than doubled . . . along the U.S.-Mexico border . . . with the largest . . . increase [in Texas].
  —Pew Research Center Spokespersons John Gramlich & Alissa Scheller, 2021

[The migrants crossing from Mexico into Texas come] from more than 105 different countries.
  —Mexican American Legal Defense/Educational Fund President Thomas Saenz, 2022

[Texas has] no authority . . . to stop illegal immigration.
  —Texas Governor Gregg Abbott, 2022

In the past two months . . . more than 3,500 unaccompanied [migrant] children [were abandoned in just one area along Texas' border].
  —Journalist Sydney Hernandez, 2020

Chapter 12

Texans pay between $31 million and $63 million to educate unaccompanied alien [migrant] children each year.
—Texas Attorney General Ken Paxton, 2022

[The migrant children at my school] put a burden on me because I've run out of space.
—Texas Principal Maria Moreno, 2014

A mayor contended that elite high schools in New York City were being forced to use a racially biased admissions test. He blamed state legislators.

State legislators contended that the Texas schools were being forced to educate more migrant students than they could handle. They blamed federal officials.

Educating Teens in NYC

Parents in New York City had for generations sent their children to private schools. They had exemplary private schools from which to choose. For example, those who sent their children to Jewish schools never doubted the quality of the education that these schools provided.

The parents who did not patronize private schools searched for exemplary public schools instead. However, they also had some remarkable public schools from which to choose. They used the term "elite" to identify them.

The parents were extremely pleased with their elite public schools. But the competition to get into them was daunting. They wished they had more of them. Parents pleaded with elected officials to establish more elite public schools, saying that they would benefit the students who attended them and act as models for the city's other schools.

The elected officials replied that they did not have the resources to create new elite schools. They urged the parents to focus their attention on the nine elite public high schools that were already operating.

The parents took the advice of the elected officials. They encouraged their children to apply to elite high schools. They were ebullient when they were admitted and were disappointed when they were not.

The disappointed parents speculated that the admissions personnel at the elite schools might have shown favoritism. They demanded an investigation. Although they could have asked their local elected officials to lead this investigation, they doubted that they would be impartial. They therefore went to their state legislators.

The legislators recognized that the parents were extremely upset. They promised to thoroughly investigate the schools.

The legislators uncovered multiple irregularities with the admission practices at elite high schools. They wished to prevent them from recurring. They came up with a plan in the early 1970s.

The legislators passed the Hecht-Calandra Act. They directed the New York City Department of Education to administer an annual academic achievement test for eighth- and ninth-grade students.

The legislators stipulated that the top-scoring students were to receive invitations to attend elite high schools. They made an exception for artistic students, who could receive invitations based on auditions or portfolios of creative work.

The legislators referred to their test as the Specialized High Schools Admissions Test (SHSAT). They were pleased when many of their constituents concluded that it was a fair way to resolve the admissions controversy.

Some constituents did not support the new admission procedure. They complained that it favored students with refined test-taking skills.

The state legislators were interested in how the New York City residents were reacting to the new admissions procedure. They were particularly interested in the mayor.

John Lindsay was mayor when the Hecht-Calandra Act was passed in 1972. He predicted that it would create an impediment for African American students. He fiercely opposed it.

Subsequent mayors continued to review the new admission procedures. Some of them shared Lindsay's disdain. Nonetheless, they recognized that the admission procedures had enhanced the prestige of the schools. Unable to come up with a credible alternative, they reluctantly allowed them to remain in place.

Bill De Blasio had campaigned for mayor in 2014 and then again four years later. During both campaigns, he pledged to combat racism.

De Blasio was upset about elite high schools. He did not question their sterling academic reputation. Nonetheless, he faulted them for using the SHSAT. He was convinced that it was a racist test.

De Blasio demanded that elite high schools create new admission procedures. He proposed that they rely on the grades that applicants had earned in elementary school.

De Blasio hoped to change the mixture of students at elite high schools. He wanted the schools to have a racial profile that mirrored that of the city's residents.

De Blasio acknowledged that his plan would reduce the number of Asian American students. However, he contended that it was worthwhile because it would increase the number of African American and Hispanic students.

Enthusiasts

De Blasio was aware of the 1970s dispute about admission procedures at elite high schools. He realized that parents, who were at the center of that dispute, were the reason for the imposition of the SHSAT. He wondered how they would react to his proposal to remove this test.

Hispanic American and African American parents had been disappointed when their children applied to elite high schools but did not get in. They predicted that their children would be more successful if the schools relied on elementary school grades. They supported the mayor's plan.

Skeptics

De Blasio was pleased that Hispanic American and African American parents supported his plan to remove the SHSAT. He hoped that Asian American parents would join them.

Asian American parents had prepared their children for the SHSAT. Some of them had personally coached them. Others had sent them to tutors. Still others had enrolled them in commercial test-preparation lessons. They were pleased when their children took the test, earned high scores, and were admitted to elite schools. They were skeptical of the mayor's plan.

De Blasio had been concerned about parents. He had shown little concern for students who were attending elite schools.

The students felt that they had been treated disdainfully. One of them, Marry Li, expressed her frustration. She asked, "Asian students like me make up the majority of those enrolled in NYC specialized high schools [and so] why was nobody asking for our input?"

The students worried that the mayor's plan would reduce the prestige of their schools. They were supported by former students who had attended esteemed universities, commenced remarkable careers, and become leaders in their communities.

The distraught parents and students reached out to journalists. They asked them to highlight their views for local, state, and national audiences.

Educating Migrants in Texas

State legislators in Texas were responsible for public schools. However, they delegated some of their most important responsibilities to the Texas Commissioner of Education, the Texas Education Agency (TEA), and the Texas State School Board of Education (SBOE).

The legislators expected the Texas Commissioner, TEA, and SBOE to establish educational policies, regularly review them, and make appropriate adaptations.

The Texas legislators kept the public schools at arm's length. They had been generally pleased with this approach. They did not wish to micromanage schools.

However, on some issues, Texas legislators had become directly involved with disputes about textbooks, tests, technology, teacher training, and school safety. In all these cases, they had been responding to the complaints of distraught constituents.

Chapter 12

The legislators had become directly involved with another problem—migrant students. They realized that this problem was particularly complex.

The legislators understood the importance of educating migrant students. They also understood the importance of securing their state's international border. They attempted to address both issues simultaneously.

The legislators had substantial control of their schools. However, they had hardly any control of their border; they depended on the United States Border Patrol (USBP) to secure it.

The USBP had the job of monitoring and protecting the nearly 1,300-mile border between Texas and Mexico. However, this agency was sparsely staffed.

The USBP had fewer than seventeen thousand agents to deploy in 2019. Although it had stationed many of them in Texas, it had to make sure that it still had enough agents to assign to the borders of other states.

The USBP agents regularly encountered people who were crossing illegally into the United States. They encountered more than 390,000 people during 2018. They encountered more than twice that number during 2019. They encountered over two million people in 2022. They noted that these people included adults and children.

Most of the migrant children were accompanied by adults. However, some were not. If the unaccompanied children had contact information for relatives in the United States, they typically were placed with them. They then attended the local public schools.

The unaccompanied children without contact information were sent to a federal emergency shelter in Texas. They then received food, clothing, medical care, and educational services. Eventually, they were placed with sponsor families and attended public schools.

The educational administrators of Texas schools did not know the residential status of their students. They explained that they were forbidden from asking the students or families this question.

Some of the educational administrators managed schools near heavily trafficked border crossing sites. Although they did not know the exact number of their students who were migrants, they assumed the number was high.

The educational administrators needed resources to handle the influx of migrant students. They pleaded for the money to hire teachers and specialized staff members. They also needed to purchase books, equipment, and school supplies.

The legislators did not doubt that the educational administrators needed resources. Nonetheless, they were not ready to supply them. They came up with an alternative plan. They would try to wrangle the resources from the federal government.

The legislators tried to persuade federal officials to supply more funds for migrant students. They explained that the federal government was responsible because it had failed to secure the Texas–Mexico border.

The legislators lost their patience. After they had been repeatedly turned down, they were ready to sue the federal government. They predicted that they would win their suit, receive a large monetary reward, and then pass this money onto the schools.

Enthusiasts

The legislators initiated their suit. They then were concerned about how parents were reacting to it.

Some parents believed that the schools were being inundated by waves of migrant students. They therefore supported the suit.

The legislators were pleased that parents approved of their suit. However, they also wanted to know how educational administrators were responding.

The educational administrators lacked the staff and resources to educate the many migrant students in their schools. They believed that federal officials had to accept the blame for this situation. They supported the suit.

Skeptics

Not all parents supported the Texas legislators. Many were skeptical.

The skeptical parents did not doubt that their legislators wished to obtain additional resources. However, they doubted that they would succeed. They urged them to be pragmatic and immediately allocate additional educational funds from their own budget.

Some educational administrators joined the skeptical parents. They doubted that the legislators would procure the federal funds they were targeting. Furthermore, they doubted that those funds, even were they to be awarded, could solve their problems.

The administrators explained that they desperately needed bilingual teachers, English as a Second Language teachers, special educators, counselors, social workers, nurses, and technology experts. They noted that a statewide shortage of these specialists would make it difficult for them to hire personnel even were salaries to become available.

Responding to Questions about Divisive Policies

Two case studies were presented in this chapter. The first one concerned parents in New York City.

These parents were proud of their city's elite public high schools. They waited each year to see if they would be ranked in the top tier of the nation's schools. They were never disappointed.

The city's mayors historically had shared the parents' pride. They had praised the elite high schools and their talented students.

Mayor Bill de Blasio had mixed feelings about these schools. He was pleased with their remarkable reputation. However, he was displeased that the students had a racial profile that did not mirror that of the city's residents.

The mayor was particularly critical that Asian American students were being admitted at a disproportionately high rate. He contrasted them with Hispanic American and African American students, who were being admitted at much lower rates. He demanded an explanation.

The administrators at the schools tried to appease the mayor. They explained that elite high schools were legally bound to employ a test-based admission process. The schools required that applicants take the SHSAT—a rigorous standardized test. They then invited those applicants with the highest scores to enroll.

The mayor was not appeased by this explanation. He still considered the admission practices to be racist. He demanded changes.

While the first case study centered on parents in New York City, the next one centered on parents in Texas. The Texans were concerned about the way statewide restrictions affected their children's schools.

State legislators were responsible for these restrictions. They or their delegates crafted them. As an example, they had imposed a restriction that prevented migrant children from enrolling in public schools. They later removed this restriction in response to pressure from the courts.

Parents were initially fine when migrant students began to enroll in the Texas public schools. However, they became concerned as their numbers grew. They feared that schools did not have the space, equipment, or staff to meet the needs of these students. They urged their legislators to deal with the problem.

The Texas legislators agreed with the parents that their schools were being overwhelmed by migrant students. They asked federal officials to supply them with additional funds. When the officials refused, they sued them.

The following questions will assist you if you are going through this book on your own. They provide opportunities like those you would have in a college class where the professor uses the case method and help if you are in an actual class using this approach.

Question 1: Why Did New York City Mayors Endorse Test-Based School Admissions?

Mayors of New York City were aware that their elite high schools were required to use a state-prescribed test to admit students. Although they were miffed, they noted that these schools were ranked among the finest in the nation. They therefore quietly endorsed the policy.

How did groups respond to the mayors? Focus on two groups: parents and students.

Did the parents have low confidence, moderate confidence, or high confidence in the way that the mayors were behaving? How did students feel? Explain the basis for your answers.

When answering these questions, as well as those that follow, you can rely on the information in this chapter. You might also use some of the sources that are identified in the references at the back of the book.

CHAPTER 12

If you are reading this chapter with a group, talk about the best way to answer the questions.

Question 2: Why Did a New York City Mayor Later Oppose Test-Based School Admissions?

Mayor De Blasio opposed the test-based school admission policy at his city's elite high schools. He explained that it created schools in which African American and Hispanic students were underrepresented. He demanded a different admission policy.

How did groups respond to this mayor? Focus on two groups: parents and students.

Did the parents have low confidence, moderate confidence, or high confidence in the way that this mayor was behaving? How did students feel? Explain the basis for your answers.

Question 3: Why Did Texas' Legislators Endorse a Court-Prescribed School Admission Policy?

Legislators in Texas were aware that their schools were required to use a court-prescribed policy to admit migrant students. Although they were miffed, they noted that the schools remained fiscally and academically sound. They therefore quietly endorsed the policy.

How did groups respond to the legislators? Focus on two groups: school administrators and parents.

Did the school administrators have low confidence, moderate confidence, or high confidence in the way that the legislators were behaving? How did the parents feel? Explain the basis for your answers.

Question 4: Why Did Texas' Legislators Later Oppose the Court-Prescribed School Admissions Policy?

Legislators in Texas later opposed the court-prescribed policy for admitting migrant students to their schools. They explained that it required schools to accept more students than they could handle. They sued the federal government for additional fiscal resources.

How did groups respond to the legislators? Focus on two groups: school administrators and parents.

Did the school administrators have low confidence, moderate confidence, or high confidence in the way that the legislators were behaving? How did the parents feel? Explain the basis for your answers.

Summary

New York City's mayor complained that elite high schools in his community were being forced to use a racially biased admissions test. He blamed state legislators and demanded they back off.

Texas legislators complained that their schools were being forced to educate more migrant students than they could handle. They blamed federal officials and demanded that they supply more money.

Bibliography

References for Preface
References for Preface Epigraphs
Charter for Compassion. (2021). Marginalized populations: Treatment of people. Retrieved from: https://charterforcompassion.org/charter-tool-box-a-framework-for-getting-started/marginalized-populations-treatment-of-people.
Gehl, N. (2109). How to better support your marginalized students. Charterforcompassion.org. Retrieved from: https://theartofeducation.edu/2019/09/02/how-to-better-support-your-marginalized-students/#:~:text=According%20to%20Charter%20For%20Compassion,women%20and%20girls.
Hannah-Jones, N. (2016, June 9). Choosing a school for my daughter in a segregated city. *New York Times*. Retrieved from: https://www.nytimes.com/2016/06/12/magazine/choosing-a-school-for-my-daughter-in-a-segregated-city.html.
Mai-Duc, C. (2022, February 15). San Francisco votes on school board recall that started with a year-plus of virtual learning. *Wall Street Journal*. Retrieved from: https://www.wsj.com/articles/san-francisco-votes-on-school-board-recall-that-started-with-a-year-plus-of-virtual-learning-11644931800.
Virginia Department of Education. (2021). Social emotional wellness considerations for youth in marginalized groups. Retrieved from: https://bestpracticesclearinghouse.ed.gov/docs/ResourcesLibrary_PDF/ED23-39c.pdf.

References for Chapter 1
References for Chapter 1 Epigraphs
DeSantis, R.—quoted by Parker, M. (2022, August 22). DeSantis endorses local school board candidates, Duval Democrats respond. News4jax.com. Retrieved from: https://www.news4jax.com/news/local/2022/08/22/duval-county-school-board-candidate-shows-favor-for-desantis-endorsing-local-candidates-duval-democrats-speak-out.
Hernández-Mats, K.—quoted by DeAngelis, C. (2022, August 28). Charlie Crist goes all in for teachers unions. *Wall Street Journal*. Retrieved from: https://www.wsj.com/articles/charles-crist-goes-all-in-for-teachers-unions-karla-hernandez-mats-american-federation-of-teachers-virginia-youngkin-desantis-closure-choice

-weingarten-governor-running-mate-11661687436?mod=hp_opin_pos_2#cxrecs_s.
Moms for Liberty. (2022). Retrieved from: https://www.momsforliberty.org.
Parents Bill of Rights. (2021). Florida State Statute 1014.02–1014.06. State of Florida. Retrieved from: http://www.leg.state.fl.us/Statutes/index.cfm?App_mode=Display_Statute&URL=1000-1099/1014/1014.html.
Parker, M. (2022, August 21). Gov. DeSantis stops in Jacksonville to tout hand-picked school board candidates, education agenda. News4jax.com. Retrieved from: https://www.news4jax.com/news/local/2022/08/21/gov-desantis-stops-in-jacksonville-to-tout-hand-picked-school-board-candidates-education-agenda.
Solochek, J. S. (2021, November 18). Florida schools react to increased parent, public participation. *Tampa Bay Times*. Retrieved from: https://www.tampabay.com/news/education/2021/11/18/florida-schools-react-to-increased-parent-public-participation.
Wall Street Journal Editorial Board. (2022, August 24). A school board revolt in Florida. *Wall Street Journal*. Retrieved from: https://www.wsj.com/articles/a-school-board-revolt-in-florida-ron-desantis-parents-districts-teachers-union-11661377688?mod=hp_opin_pos_2#cxrecs_s.

References for Empowered Police—Introduction
2021 Florida Statutes 943.1718. Body cameras; policies and procedures. Leg.state.fl.us. Retrieved from: http://www.leg.state.fl.us/statutes/index.cfm?App_mode=Display_Statute&URL=0900-0999/0943/Sections/0943.1718.html.
Marsy's Law crime victim rights. (2021, December). Ballotpedia.org. Retrieved from: https://ballotpedia.org/Marsy%27s_Law_crime_victim_rights.
Marsy's Law for Florida (2021). About Marsy's Law. Marsyslawforfl.com. Retrieved from: https://www.marsyslawforfl.com/about_marsys_law.

References for Empowered Police—Enthusiasts
Marsey, J. D. (2021, April 8). On-duty law enforcement officers are entitled to invoke Marsy's Law victim confidentiality. Jdsupra.com. Retrieved from: https://www.jdsupra.com/legalnews/on-duty-law-enforcement-officers-are-4672302.

References for Empowered Police—Skeptics
Downey, R. (2022, May 12). Gov. DeSantis signs bill fortifying rights for crime victims. Floridapolitics.com. Retrieved from: https://floridapolitics.com/archives/524491-gov-desantis-signs-bill-fortifying-rights-for-crime-victims.
Florida Supreme Court. (2022, March 20). City of Tallahassee v. Florida Police Benevolent Association, Inc. Rcfp.org. Retrieved from: https://www.rcfp.org/briefs-comments/tallahassee-v-florida-police-union.
Hope, A. (2022, February 3). Marsy's Law debate: Are officers victims if they get threatened? Wesh.com. Retrieved from: https://www.wesh.com/article/marsys

-law-debate-are-officers-victims-if-they-get-threatened-case-heads-to-florida-supreme-court/38966507#.
Rivero, D. (2021, April 8). "Marsy's Law" ruling makes police "accountability nearly impossible" in Florida, says first amendment group. Wlrn.org/news. Retrieved from: https://www.wlrn.org/news/2021-04-08/ruling-makes-police-accountability-nearly-impossible-in-florida-says-first-amendment-foundation.
Sachs, S. (2021, December 22). Marsy's Law: Florida Supreme Court to decide if police officers are victims of crimes. Wfla.com/news. Retrieved from: https://www.wfla.com/news/florida/marsys-law-florida-supreme-court-to-decide-if-police-officers-are-victims-of-crimes.
Tallahassee police "Marsy's Law" dispute goes to Florida Supreme Court. (2021, May 5). Wfsu.org. Retrieved from: https://news.wfsu.org/wfsu-local-news/2021-05-05/tallahassee-police-marsys-law-dispute-goes-to-florida-supreme-court.
TCPalm Editorial Board. (2022, April 29). Law enforcement officers shouldn't use Marsy's Law to hide public information. Tcpalm.com. Retrieved from: https://www.tcpalm.com/story/opinion/2022/04/29/marsys-law-should-protect-victims-not-police-officers-our-view/9559475002.

References for Empowered Parents—Introduction

Anderson, Z., & Brugal, S. (2021, December 14). Moms for Liberty. *Florida Times-Union*. Retrieved from: https://jacksonville-fl-app.newsmemory.com/?publink=2e37437bb_1346032.
Dailey, R. (2021, July 13). School standards targeted for revisions. *Florida Times—Union*. Retrieved from: https://www.mysuncoast.com/2021/07/13/school-standards-targeted-revisions.
Di Gregorio, R. (2021, June 11). What will Florida's ban on Critical Race Theory change in schools? Firstcoastnews.com. Retrieved from: https://www.firstcoastnews.com/article/entertainment/television/programs/gmj/what-will-floridas-ban-on-critical-race-theory-change-in-schools/77-0051072d-b692-4670-9663-f568fa7227b7.
Downey, M. (2021, October 31). Opinion: School boards under siege. *Atlanta Journal-Constitution*. Retrieved from: https://www.ajc.com/education/get-schooled-blog/opinion-school-boards-under-siege/H6OJHKD4KRF3BAEEPPHA4YC2TY/?outputType=amp csc.
Feindt, C. (2021, June 10). Florida votes to keep "Critical Race Theory" out of the classroom. Firstcoastnews.com. Retrieved from: https://www.firstcoastnews.com/article/news/education/local-activists-protest-ahead-of-florida-state-board-of-education-critical-race-theory-vote/77-bc81c9ce-98a0-43c7-a45a-16e66bfbd3a1.
Giordano, G. (2003). *Twentieth-century textbook wars: A history of advocacy and opposition.* New York: P. Lang.
Giordano, G. (2019). *Parents and textbooks: Answers that reveal essential steps for improvement.* Lanham, MD: Rowman & Littlefield.
Henninger, D. (2021, July 7). Welcome to the equity war. *Wall Street Journal.* Retrieved from: https://www.wsj.com/articles/welcome-to-the-equity-war-11625696029?mod=trending_now_opn_2.

McGurn, W. (2021, October 11). Virginia dad takes on the school board. *Wall Street Journal.* Retrieved from: https://www.wsj.com/articles/harry-jackson-school-board-fairfax-virginia-education-fbi-nsba-justice-department-11633985271?mod=hp_opin_pos_4#cxrecs_s.

Mai-Duc, C. (2021, November 27). In San Francisco, parent anger focuses on school board recall. *Wall Street Journal.* Retrieved from: https://www.wsj.com/articles/in-san-francisco-parent-anger-focuses-on-school-board-recall-11638025202?mod=hp_lead_pos9.

Mervosh, S., & Heyward, G. (2021, August 18). The school culture wars: "You have brought division to us." *New York Times.* Retrieved from: https://www.nytimes.com/2021/08/18/us/schools-covid-critical-race-theory-masks-gender.html.

Miller, R. W. (2021, July 3). Shouting matches, arrests and fed up parents: How school board meetings became ground zero in politics. *USA TODAY.* Retrieved from: https://www.usatoday.com/story/news/education/2021/07/03/critical-race-theory-makes-school-board-meetings-political-ground-zero/7785802002.

Souza, A., & Souza, S. (2021, November 15). Critical race theory wasn't the only reason we pulled our daughter from her school. *AZcentral.com.* Retrieved from: https://www.azcentral.com/story/opinion/op-ed/2021/11/15/critical-race-theory-one-reason-pulled-daughter-peoria-school/8592329002/.

Zhang, T. (2021, July 15). Is Critical Race Theory the best way to teach students history, racism? *Florida Times-Union.* Retrieved from: https://www.jacksonville.com/story/opinion/columns/guest/2021/07/15/critical-race-theory-best-way-teach-history-and-racism/7871649002.

References for Empowered Parents—Enthusiasts

Allen, K. (2021, June 20). Policy won't stop discussion about racism. *Florida Times-Union.* Retrieved from: https://jacksonville-fl-app.newsmemory.com/?publink=12e8e6be7_1345de0.

Anderson, Z., & Walker, S. (2022, August 23). DeSantis boosts school board races. *Florida Times-Union.* Retrieved from: https://jacksonville-fl-app.newsmemory.com/?publink=00eda01a3_13485bb.

Bloch, E. (2021, June 10). Florida Board of Education approves new academic standards opposing Critical Race Theory. *Florida Times-Union.* Retrieved from: https://www.jacksonville.com/story/news/education/2021/06/10/state-approves-strict-teaching-standards-opposing-critical-race-theory/7621918002.

Bloch, E., Richards, E., Stern, G., & Fernando. C. (2021, December 8). Is math education racist? *Florida Times-Union.* Retrieved from: https://jacksonville-fl-app.newsmemory.com/?publink=353b9966b_134602c.

Cokley, K. (2021, July 7). Teaching critical race theory reminds us systemic racism still exists—That's not anti-American. *USA TODAY.* Retrieved from: https://www.usatoday.com/story/opinion/voices/2021/07/06/systemic-racism-pervasive-critical-race-theory-reminder/5336313001.

Daytona Beach News-Journal Editorial Board. (2021, June 15). Florida's new "critical race theory" rule might backfire on DeSantis and conservatives. *Daytona*

Beach News-Journal. Retrieved from: https://www.news-journalonline.com/story/opinion/editorials/2021/06/15/critical-race-theory-rule-might-backfire-desantis-conservatives/7660472002.

Hannah-Jones, N., Roper, C., Silverman, I., & Silverstein, J. (Eds.). (2021). *The 1619 project: A new origin story.* New York: New York Times/One World.

Jackson, L. (2021, August 18). What is Critical Race Theory? *New York Times.* Retrieved from: https://www.nytimes.com/2021/07/09/podcasts/the-daily-newsletter-critical-race-theory.html.

Photos: DCPS board meeting support, protest. (2022, May 4). *Florida Times-Union.* Retrieved from: https://www.jacksonville.com/picture-gallery/news/2022/05/04/dcps-board-meeting-support-protest/9645695002.

Schnell, L. (2021, June 14). "Laws in search of problems that don't exist": Republicans try to ban critical race theory in colleges. *USA TODAY.* Retrieved from: https://www.usatoday.com/in-depth/news/education/2021/06/13/republicans-want-critical-race-theory-out-college-classes-too/7621012002.

References for Empowered Parents—Skeptics

Algar, S. (2021, December 14). New proposal would allow DOE to boot parents from education panels. *New York Post.* Retrieved from: https://nypost.com/2021/12/14/new-proposal-would-allow-doe-to-boot-parents-from-education-panels.

Ault, N., & Keller, M. (2022, September 2). How teachers are secretly taught critical race theory. *Wall Street Journal.* Retrieved from: https://www.wsj.com/articles/if-students-dont-learn-critical-race-theory-why-do-teachers-pacific-educational-group-school-board-administrators-students-class-11662150413.

Bloomberg, M. R. (2022, August 15). Republican censorship goes for woke. *Wall Street Journal.* Retrieved from: https://www.wsj.com/articles/republican-censors-go-for-woke-florida-ron-desantis-critical-race-theory-ban-gender-universities-businesses-training-dei-free-expression-11660595313?mod=article_inline.

Commonwealth of Virginia Office of the Governor. (2022). Executive Order number one (2022): Ending the use of inherently divisive concepts, including critical race theory, and restoring excellence in K-12 public education in the commonwealth. Author. Retrieved from: chrome-extension://efaidnbmnnnibpcajpcglclefindmkaj/viewer.html?pdfurl=https%3A%2F%2Fs.wsj.net%2Fpublic%2Fresources%2Fdocuments%2FVirginia_Executive_Order_1.pdf&clen=321922&chunk=true.

Conklin, A. (2021, December 4). National School Boards Association fallout continues as half of US states push back against organization. Foxnews.com. Retrieved from: https://www.foxnews.com/politics/states-leaving-national-school-board-association.

Freeman, J. (2021, October 6). Students in a "hostile environment." *Wall Street Journal.* Retrieved from: https://www.wsj.com/articles/students-in-a-hostile-environment-11633557732.

Galston, W. A. (2021, July 20). A deeper look at Critical Race Theory. *Wall Street Journal.* Retrieved from: https://www.wsj.com/articles/kimberle-crenshaw-critical-race-theory-woke-marxism-education-11626793272.

Morrow, L. (2021, July 19). The hedgehogs of Critical Race Theory. *Wall Street Journal*. Retrieved from: https://www.wsj.com/articles/isaiah-berlin-critical-race-theory-progressives-woke-culture-wars-marxism-11626724499?mod=hp_opin_pos_2.

Myler, P. (2022, August 24). Why do we send teachers for re-education? [Letter-to-the-Editor]. *Wall Street Journal*. Retrieved from: https://www.wsj.com/articles/teacher-education-school-critical-theory-college-requirement-certification-11661291521?cx_testId=3&cx_testVariant=cx_4&cx_artPos=1&mod=WTRN#cxrecs_s.

Noonan, P. (2021, November 4). Voters give Democrats a woke-up call. *Wall Street Journal*. Retrieved from: https://www.wsj.com/articles/voters-give-democrats-a-woke-up-call-republicans-youngkin-virginia-progressives-11636059748?mod=hp_opin_pos_4#cxrecs_s.

Noonan, P. (2021, November 11). Democrats need to face down the woke. *Wall Street Journal*. Retrieved from: https://www.wsj.com/articles/voters-give-democrats-a-woke-up-call-republicans-youngkin-virginia-progressives-11636059748?mod=hp_opin_pos_4#cxrecs_s.

O'Neil, T. (2021, November 9). Loudoun School Board meeting erupts into shouting as parent group files petition to oust board chair. Foxnews.com. Retrieved from: https://www.foxnews.com/us/loudoun-school-board-meeting-erupts-into-shouting-as-parent-group-files-petition-to-oust-board-chair.

Patterson, S. (2022, August 25). Carney, Joyce win school board seats. Newsmemory.com. Retrieved from: https://jacksonville-fl-app.newsmemory.com/?publink=0adef937f_13485bd.

Peoples, S. (2021, November 5). In Virginia, GOP finds new playbook: Not easily replicated. APnews.com. Retrieved from: https://apnews.com/article/election-2021-analysis-virginia-governor-youngkin-c78b860c08a2e7dfa4eba24cd1dc384e.

Raleigh, H. (2021, December 8). Woke math education reform is too dangerous to ignore. *News Week*. Retrieved from: https://www.newsweek.com/woke-math-education-reform-too-dangerous-ignore-opinion-1656527.

Riley, J. L. (2021, July 13). Critical Race Theory is a hustle. *Wall Street Journal*. Retrieved from: https://www.wsj.com/articles/critical-race-theory-is-a-hustle-11626214782?mod=hp_opin_pos_3.

Rufo, C. F. (2021, June 27). Battle over critical race theory. *Wall Street Journal*. Retrieved from: https://www.wsj.com/articles/battle-over-critical-race-theory-11624810791?mod=hp_opin_pos_1.

Sartoris, K. (2021, December 16). DeSantis unveils "Stop WOKE Act" in The Villages. *Florida Times-Union*. Retrieved from: https://jacksonville-fl-app.newsmemory.com/?publink=0fce0cdf9_1346034.

Siders, D., Fineout, G., & Dixon, M. (2022, August 24). Democrats gain momentum: 5 takeaways from the last big primary night of 2022. Politico.com. Retrieved from: https://www.politico.com/news/2022/08/24/5-takeaways-as-the-2022-primary-season-winds-down-00053445.

Solochek, J. S. (2021, April 6). Florida Republicans see education policy as their election edge. *Tampa Bay Times*. Retrieved from: https://www.tampabay.com/news/

education/2022/04/06/florida-republicans-see-education-policy-as-their-election-edge.

Wall Street Journal Editorial Board. (2021, July 7). The teachers [*sic*] unions go woke. *Wall Street Journal.* Retrieved from: https://www.wsj.com/articles/the-teachers-unions-go-woke-11625697757?mod=hp_opin_pos_1.

Wall Street Journal Editorial Board. (2021, July 18). Critical Race Theory runs into parents. [Video]. *Wall Street Journal.* Retrieved from: https://www.wsj.com/video/series/journal-editorial-report/wsj-opinion-critical-race-theory-runs-into-parents/EEF5ECC7-746D-4EF7-AFBF-96522FC9A4FF.

Wall Street Journal Editorial Board. (2021, October 14). Education horror show, continued. *Wall Street Journal.* Retrieved from: https://www.wsj.com/articles/education-horror-show-continued-ramona-bessinger-providence-public-school-district-critical-race-theory-11634250506?mod=hp_opin_pos_6#cxrecs_s.

Wall Street Journal Editorial Board. (2021, December 5). Squaring up to defend mathematics. *Wall Street Journal.* Retrieved from: https://www.wsj.com/articles/defending-mathematics-science-stem-equity-education-california-k12-math-matters-11638728196?mod=hp_trending_now_opn_pos4.

Wall Street Journal Editorial Board. (2022, August 24). A school board revolt in Florida. *Wall Street Journal.* Retrieved from: https://www.wsj.com/articles/a-school-board-revolt-in-florida-ron-desantis-parents-districts-teachers-union-11661377688?mod=hp_opin_pos_2#cxrecs_s.

REFERENCES FOR CHAPTER 2
References for Chapter 2 Epigraphs

Florida *Fairness in Women's Sports Act.* (2022). Fla. Stat. § 1006.205. Florida-Statutes. Retrieved from: https://casetext.com/statute/florida-statutes/title-xlviii-early-learning-20-education-code/chapter-1006-support-for-learning/part-i-public-k-12-education-support-for-learning-and-student-services/student-extracurricular-activities-and-athletics/section-1006205-fairness-in-womens-sports-act.

Florida High School Athletic Association.—quoted by Transathlete.com. (2022). K-12 policies. Transathlete.com. Retrieved from: https://www.transathlete.com/k-12#:~:text=The%20Florida%20High%20School%20Athletic,the%20gender%20listed%20on%20a.

DeSantis, R. (2021, June 2). DeSantis defends transgender athletes bill: We have to protect our girls [video]. Foxnews.com. Retrieved from: https://www.foxnews.com/media/desantis-transgender-athletes-bill-protect-girls.

Johns, M. (2019, January 25). Transgender identity experiences of violence victimization, substance use, suicide risk, and sexual risk behaviors among high school students—19 states and large urban school districts, 2017. CDC.gov. Retrieved from: https://www.cdc.gov/mmwr/volumes/68/wr/mm6803a3.htm#.

Oakley, C.—quoted by Blad, E. (2021, October 22). Transgender students and school sports: Six things to know about a raging debate. *Education Week.* Retrieved from: https://www.edweek.org/leadership/transgender-students-and-school-sports-six-things-to-know-about-a-raging-debate/2021/10.

Paley, A.—quoted by Rezal, A. (2021, December 1). States restricting how transgender students play sports. Usnews.com. Retrieved from: https://www.usnews.com/news/best-states/articles/2021-12-01/these-states-restrict-how-transgender-students-participate-in-school-sports.

Platt Rady, K. (2021, April 20). Florida legislature proposes bill banning transgender school/college athletes from girls' & women's sports. Jdsupra.com. Retrieved from: https://www.jdsupra.com/legalnews/florida-legislature-proposes-bill-9100615.

References for Banning Facebook Users—Introduction

Lee, D. (2019, May 3). Facebook bans "dangerous individuals." Bbc.com. Retrieved from: https://www.bbc.com/news/technology-48142098.

Holzberg, M. (2021, March 22). Facebook banned 1.3 billion accounts over three months to combat "fake" and "harmful" content. Forbes.com. Retrieved from: https://www.forbes.com/sites/melissaholzberg/2021/03/22/facebook-banned-13-billion-accounts-over-three-months-to-combat-fake-and-harmful-content/?sh=167771305215.

Ray, S. (2021, March 15). Facebook will add labels to all posts about covid-19 vaccines that will promote "authoritative information." Forbes.com. Retrieved from: https://www.forbes.com/sites/siladityaray/2021/03/15/facebook-will-add-labels-to-all-posts-about-covid-19-vaccines-that-will-promote-authoritative-information/?sh=126869a87cb8.

References for Banning Facebook Users—Enthusiasts

Facebook Oversight Board. (2021, May). Oversight Board upholds former President Trump's suspension, finds Facebook failed to impose proper penalty. Oversightboard.com. Retrieved from: https://oversightboard.com/news/226612455899839-oversight-board-upholds-former-president-trump-s-suspension-finds-facebook-failed-to-impose-proper-penalty.

Horwitz, J. (2021, September 13). Facebook says its rules apply to all. *Wall Street Journal*. Retrieved from: https://www.wsj.com/articles/facebook-files-xcheck-zuckerberg-elite-rules-11631541353?mod=series_facebookfiles.

Levy, S. (2021). *Facebook: The inside story*. UK: Penguin Business.

References for Banning Facebook Users—Skeptics

Bender M. C., & Wells, G. (2022, January 9). How the Trump social-media ban paid off for Trump, platforms. *Wall Street Journal*. Retrieved from: https://www.wsj.com/articles/how-the-trump-social-media-ban-paid-off-for-trump-platforms-11641729604.

Bengali, S. (2021, January 15). Facebook banned Trump but has failed to react quickly to other leaders who incited violence. *Los Angeles Times*. Retrieved from: https://www.latimes.com/world-nation/story/2021-01-15/facebook-social-media-bans-trump-capitol-riot.

Hagey, K., & Horwitz, J. (2021, September 15). Facebook tried to make its platform a healthier place: It got angrier instead. *Wall Street Journal.* Retrieved from: https://www.wsj.com/articles/facebook-algorithm-change-zuckerberg-11631654215?mod=series_facebookfiles.

Hill, K. (2019, November 22). Many are abandoning Facebook. *New York Times.* Retrieved from: https://www.nytimes.com/2019/08/22/business/reactivate-facebook-account.html.

Horwitz, J. et al. (2021, September 13). The Facebook files, part 1: The whitelist [audiophile]. *Wall Street Journal.* Retrieved from: https://www.wsj.com/podcasts/the-journal/the-facebook-files-part-1-the-whitelist/72a1e8f5-a187-4a91-bedb-b0b0d39f5cce.

Hotham, T. (2020, October 8). Trump v Biden: Who is engaging the most followers on Facebook? Theconversation.com. Retrieved from: https://theconversation.com/trump-v-biden-who-is-engaging-the-most-followers-on-facebook-146520.

Ohm, R. (2020, March 5). Trump's Truth Social launches on Apple's App store, with glitches. *Wall Street Journal.* Retrieved from: https://www.wsj.com/articles/trumps-truth-social-launches-with-glitches-11645528246?mod=hp_lead_pos7.

Scheck, J., Purnell, N., & Horwitz, J. (2021, September 16). Facebook employees flag drug cartels and human traffickers. *Wall Street Journal.* Retrieved from: https://www.wsj.com/articles/facebook-drug-cartels-human-traffickers-response-is-weak-documents-11631812953.

Wall Street Journal. Why would Instagram make its product less addictive [Blog]. (2021, September 28). Retrieved from: https://www.wsj.com/articles/instagram-product-less-addictive-social-media-image-11632861506.

Wells, G., Horwitz, J., & Seetharaman, D. (2021, September 14). Facebook knows Instagram is toxic for teen girls, company documents show. *Wall Street Journal.* Retrieved from: https://www.wsj.com/articles/facebook-knows-instagram-is-toxic-for-teen-girls-company-documents-show-11631620739.

References for Banning Transgender Athletes—Introduction

Alfonseca, K. (2022, February 4). South Dakota signs 1st anti-transgender sports law of 2022. Abcnews.go.com. Retrieved from: https://abcnews.go.com/US/south-dakota-signs-1st-anti-transgender-sports-law/story?id=82672739.

Barnes, K. (2021, September 1). Young transgender athletes caught in middle of states' debates. Espn.com. Retrieved from: https://www.espn.com/espn/story/_/id/32115820/young-transgender-athletes-caught-middle-states-debates.

BBC.com. (2019, March 2). Sharron Davies: Former British swimmer says transgender athletes should not compete in women's sport. Retrieved from: https://www.bbc.com/sport/swimming/47428951.amp.

Blanchet, B. (2022, February 6). 16 UPenn swimmers issue letter supporting rule that would prevent transgender teammate Lia Thomas from competing. Yahoo.com. Retrieved from: https://news.yahoo.com/16-upenn-swimmers-issue-letter-234552644.html.

D'Addona, D. (2022, March 9). Lia Thomas teammate: Situation is "unfair" and NCAA is "discriminating against cisgender women"; Locker room discomfort. Swimmingworldmagazine.com. Retrieved from: https://www.swimmingworldmagazine.com/news/lia-thomas-teammate-situation-is-unfair-and-ncaa-is-discriminating-against-cisgender-women-locker-room-discomfort.

Gaydos, R. (2022, January 7). Lia Thomas finds support from Penn, Ivy League ahead of weekend meet. *Fox News*. Retrieved from: https://www.foxnews.com/sports/lia-thomas-support-penn-ivy-league-weekend-meet.

Gaydos, R. (2022, January 17). Thomas wasn't as dominant in her latest tri-meet. *Fox News*. Retrieved from: https://www.foxnews.com/sports/lia-thomas-comparing-jackie-robinson.

Higgins, L. (2021, July 1). Blocked from her signature race, caster Semenya won't run in Tokyo. *Wall Street Journal*. Retrieved from: https://www.wsj.com/articles/caster-semenya-tokyo-olympics-11625159284.

Nelson, J. Q. (2022, January 20). Caitlyn Jenner: "Woke world" not working for women's sports. *Fox News*. Retrieved from: https://www.foxnews.com/media/caitlyn-jenner-biological-boys-should-not-be-playing-in-womens-sports.

U.S. Department of Justice. (2022). TITLE IX. Retrieved from: https://www.justice.gov/crt/title-ix.

Witz, B. (2022, January 24). As Lia Thomas swims, debate about transgender athletes swirls. *New York Times*. Retrieved from: https://www.nytimes.com/2022/01/24/sports/lia-thomas-transgender-swimmer.html.

References for Banning Transgender Athletes—Enthusiasts

Eaton-Robb, P. (2020, February 12). Girls sue to block participation of transgender athletes. Abcnews.go.com. Retrieved from: https://abcnews.go.com/Sports/wireStory/girls-sue-block-participation-transgender-athletes-68941543.

The Guardian. (2020, February 13). Teen runners sue to block trans athletes from girls' sports. Retrieved from: https://www.theguardian.com/us-news/2020/feb/13/transgender-athletes-girls-sports-high-school.

Levinovitz, A. (2021, August 5). A level playing field for transgender athletes. *Wall Street Journal*. Retrieved from: https://www.wsj.com/articles/a-level-playing-field-for-transgender-athletes-11628183000?

McCarthy, J. (2021, May 26). Mixed views among Americans on transgender issues. Gallup.com. Retrieved from: https://news.gallup.com/poll/350174/mixed-views-among-americans-transgender-issues.aspx.

Maxouris, C. (2020, February 14). 3 Connecticut high school girls are suing over a policy that allows trans athletes to compete in girls' sports. Cnn.com. Retrieved from: https://www.cnn.com/2020/02/14/us/transgender-athletes-connecticut-lawsuit/index.html.

Shrier, A. (2021, January 22). Joe Biden's first day began the end of girls' sports. *Wall Street Journal*. Retrieved from: https://www.wsj.com/articles/joe-bidens-first-day-began-the-end-of-girls-sports-11611341066.

BIBLIOGRAPHY

References for Banning Transgender Athletes—Skeptics

Barnes, K. (2022, March 15). Advocacy groups ask policymakers to prioritize fairness for biological women in sport. Espn.com. Retrieved from: https://www.espn.com/olympics/story/_/id/33511880/advocacy-groups-ask-congress-sports-governing-bodies-prioritize-fairness-biological-women.

Bianchi, M. (2021, April 16). Why are Florida politicians trying to ban transgender athletes who aren't even a problem? *Orlando Sentinel*. Retrieved from: https://www.orlandosentinel.com/sports/mike-bianchi-commentary/os-sp-transgender-female-sports-athletes-florida-20210416-jyfzy5jmenarbplty4ieyuxfuu-story.html.

Magowan, A. (2018, December 18). Transgender women in sport: Are they really a "threat" to female sport? Bbc.com. Retrieved from: https://www.bbc.com/sport/46453958.

NBCNews.com. (2021, February 24). Biden administration withdraws from transgender athlete case. Retrieved from: https://www.nbcnews.com/feature/nbc-out/biden-administration-withdraws-transgender-athlete-case-n1258723.

Sosin, K. (2021, May 26). Gallup finds Americans oppose transgender sports participation, challenging past polling. 19thnews.org. Retrieved from: https://19thnews.org/2021/05/gallup-americans-oppose-transgender-sports-participation.

Walsh, M. (2021, February 24). Biden legal team steps back from Trump stance on transgender female sports participation. *Education Week*. Retrieved from: https://www.edweek.org/policy-politics/biden-legal-team-steps-back-from-trump-stance-on-transgender-female-sports-participation/2021/02.

REFERENCES FOR CHAPTER 3
References for Chapter 3 Epigraphs

Albuquerque Public Schools. (2022). Student dress. Aps.edu. Retrieved from: https://www.aps.edu/about-us/policies-and-procedural-directives/procedural-directives/j.-students/student-dress.

Bloch, E. (2022, May 22). "My skin isn't distracting": Students dish on dress code. *Florida Times-Union*. Retrieved from: https://jacksonville-fl-app.newsmemory.com/?publink=364076215_134848e.

Bryant, A., & Mardis, J.—quoted by Downey, M. (2021, October 3). What does it say to a 10-year-old when her body is routinely measured and critiqued? *Atlanta Journal-Constitution*. Retrieved from: https://www.ajc.com/education/get-schooled-blog/dress-codes-what-does-it-say-to-a-10-year-old-when-her-body-is-routinely-measured-and-critiqued/RXQPUVHPJ5EVVL34LKJ27HGZVQ/.

Duval County Public Schools. (2022). Student dress code. Retrieved from: https://dcps.duvalschools.org/domain/1306.

Gresham-Barlow School District. (2022). Dress code. Gresham.k12.or. Retrieved from: https://www.gresham.k12.or.us/cms/lib/OR02216641/Centricity/Domain/1613/Dress_Code_Revised_2015.pdf.

Bibliography

Joseph, J. (2021, December 9). High school boys wear crop tops to class to expose sexist dress code double standards. Scoop.upworthy.com. Retrieved from: https://scoop.upworthy.com/boys-wear-crop-tops-to-school-protest-sexist-dress-code.

National Women's Law Center.—quoted by Jones, S. (2018, August 31). Do School dress codes discriminate against girls? *Education Week*. Retrieved from: https://www.edweek.org/leadership/do-school-dress-codes-discriminate-against-girls/2018/08.

Thompson, N.—quoted by Rivas, M. (2019, September 27). It's time to retire school dress codes. Parents.com. Retrieved from: https://www.parents.com/kids/teens/its-time-to-retire-school-dress-codes.

References for Dress Codes for Athletes—Introduction

Pruitt-Young, S. (2021, July 23). The sexualization of women in sports extends even to what they wear. Npr.org. Retrieved from: https://www.npr.org/2021/07/23/1019343453/women-sports-sexualization-uniforms-problem.

Tokyo Olympics: Female athletes face double standards over uniforms. (2021, July 22). France24.com. Retrieved from: https://www.france24.com/en/sport/20210722-tokyo-olympics-female-athletes-face-double-standards-over-uniforms.

References for Dress Codes for Athletes—Enthusiasts

European Handball Federation. (2022). Beach handball history. Retrieved from: https://beach.eurohandball.com/about-beach-handball/beach-handball-history.

Handbollskanalen.se. (2021, November 10). New rules in beach handball: Men to play in shorts—women in hotpants. Retrieved from: https://handbollskanalen.se/beachhandboll/new-rules-in-beach-handball-men-to-play-in-shorts-women-in-hotpants/.

International Handball Federation. (2014). IX Rules of the Game. Author. t/ix-rules-of-the-game-international-handball-federation-rules-of-the-game-beach.html?page=1.

References for Dress Codes for Athletes—Skeptics

Radnofsky, C. (2021, November 1). Norway's beach handball team wins fight over sexist uniform rules. Nbcnews.com. Retrieved from: https://www.nbcnews.com/news/world/norways-beach-handball-team-win-fight-sexist-uniform-rules-rcna4218.

Satran, R. (2021, July 31). Bye-bye bikinis: Athletes at the Olympics and beyond fight sexist uniforms. *Wall Street Journal*. Retrieved from: https://www.wsj.com/articles/bye-bye-bikinis-athletes-at-the-olympics-and-beyond-fight-sexist-uniforms-11627684035?mod=trending_now_news_pos4.

Woodyatt, A. (2021, July 31). For years, female athletes have had their clothing policed: Now, they're fighting back. Cnn.com. Retrieved from: https://www.cnn.com/style/article/female-athlete-clothing-olympics/index.html.

Bibliography

References for Dress Codes for Students—Introduction

Barbella, M. (2020, October 20). School dress codes present double standard. New Jersey State Bar Foundation. Retrieved from: https://njsbf.org/2020/10/20/school-dress-codes-present-double-standard.

Bily, C. A. (2016). *Dress codes in schools.* New York: Rosen.

Chastaine, D. (2019, September 6). Parents successfully fight against "sexist" dress code. Covingtonreporter.com. Retrieved from: https://www.covingtonreporter.com/news/parents-successfully-fight-against-sexist-dress-code.

Espejo, R. (2012). *Dress.* Detroit: Greenhaven.

Fossey R. & DeMitchell, T. A. (2014). Student dress codes and the first amendment: Legal challenges and policy issues. Lanham, MD: Rowman & Littlefield.

Hamilton, J. (2016). *Dress codes in schools.* New York: Rosen.

Hudson, D. L. (2014). *Let the students speak: A history of the fight for free expression in American schools.* Boston: Beacon.

Kawa, K. (2018). *Are school uniforms good for students?* Detroit: Greenhaven.

Khan, A. (2022, September 1). DC area parents debate in private online groups over school dress codes for students. Fox5dc.com. Retrieved from: https://www.fox5dc.com/news/dc-area-parents-debate-in-private-online-groups-over-school-dress-codes-for-students.

Frazier, K. (2022). Typical school dress codes. Teens.lovetoknow.com. Retrieved from: https://teens.lovetoknow.com/School_Dress_Codes.

Nittle, N. (2019, May 7). A high school's dress code for parents sparked backlash: The principal is standing by it. Vox.com. Retrieved from: https://www.vox.com/the-goods/2019/5/7/18532416/james-madison-high-school-dress-code.

Owens, L. (2021). *Should schools have dress codes?* Detroit: Greenhaven.

Socorro Independent School District. (2022). Stallion dress code. Author. Retrieved from: https://www.sisd.net/domain/1771.

References for Dress Codes for Students—Enthusiasts

Cruz, I. (2018, September 15). Parents against dress codes: 20 ways parents (and their kids) fought back. Moms.com. Retrieved from: https://www.moms.com/parents-against-dress-codes-20-ways-parents-and-their-kids-fought-back.

Dalton, M. (2021, December 12). In France, criticism grows over U.S.-inspired activism on race, gender. *Wall Street Journal.* Retrieved from: https://www.wsj.com/articles/in-france-criticism-grows-over-u-s-inspired-activism-on-race-gender-11639319941.

Educators4sc.org. (2022). Teaching with dress code restrictions. Retrieved from: https://educators4sc.org/classroom-practices/teaching-with-dress-code-restrictions.

Miller, D. (2022, August 29). "No More Sagging" campaign offers free belts to high school students with sagging pants. Fox29.com. Retrieved from: https://www.fox29.com/news/free-belts-high-school-students-campaign.

Rammohan, Y. (2012, May 31). Controversy arises over saggy pants in school. Wttw.com. Retrieved from: https://news.wttw.com/2012/05/31/controversy-arises-over-saggy-pants-school.

Bibliography

Shannon, J. (2019, April 23). Texas school's dress code for parents bans "sagging pants," pajamas, hair rollers and more. *Herald-Mail*. Retrieved from: https://www.heraldmailmedia.com/story/news/2019/04/24/exas-schools-dress-code-for-parents-bans-sagging-pants-pajamas-hair-rollers-and-more/44304933.

References for Dress Codes for Students—Skeptics

Harbach, M. J. (2015). Sexualization, sex discrimination, and public school dress codes. *University of Richmond Law Review*. Retrieved from: https://heinonline.org/hol-cgi-bin/get_pdf.cgihandle=hein.journals/urich50&section=38&casa_token=Zb1sVcuTzK0AAAAA:VQ1pHRZz5AiJ0GdkRWLhukipIvx1iQCmaV0DtuKdWkqxBiPXOWYCnBsFCeo7eS-ZP0qLqLM.

Jones, C. M. (2021, July 28). St. Johns County School Board proposes more gender-neutral dress code for new school year. *St. Augustine Record*. Retrieved from: https://www.staugustine.com/story/news/education/2021/07/28/st-johns-county-school-district-proposes-more-gender-neutral-dress-code/5388699001/.

Jones, S. (2018, August 31). Do school dress codes discriminate against girls? *Education Week*. Retrieved from: https://www.edweek.org/leadership/do-school-dress-codes-discriminate-against-girls/2018/08.

McClellan, J. (2018, August 21). California school's no-shame dress code empowers students to wear what they want. *USA TODAY*. Retrieved from: https://www.usatoday.com/story/life/allthemoms/2018/08/21/san-francisco-bay-area-schools-no-shame-dress-code-allows-tube-tops-and-torn-jeans/1052718002.

McLean, J. (2021, May 21). St. Johns school district offers refunds after female student photos edited in yearbook for dress code violations. News4jax.com. Retrieved from: https://www.news4jax.com/news/local/2021/05/20/st-johns-school-district-offers-refunds-after-female-student-photos-edited-in-yearbook-for-code-violations/.

McLean, J. (2021, May 22). 80 yearbook photos, all girls, edited by St. Johns County high school employee. News4jax.com. Retrieved from: https://www.news4jax.com/news/local/2021/05/21/80-yearbook-photos-all-females-edited-by-st-johns-county-high-school-employee/.

McLean, J. (2021, May 24). Florida high school alters 80 "immodest" yearbook photos of students. Bbc.com. Retrieved from: https://www.bbc.com/news/world-us-canada-57232694.

Whitman, G. M. (2020). A curricular critique of school dress codes. *Clearing House*. Retrieved from: https://www.tandfonline.com/doi/abs/10.1080/00098655.2020.1721415.

Zimmerman, J. (2021, October 1). Fear, loathing, and dress codes in American schools. Dividedwefall.org. Retrieved from: https://dividedwefall.org/dress-codes/?gclid=CjwKCAjwvNaYBhA3EiwACgndgklC8-_mVGwBHr5YCfaeFnw2Nmx7k9Ra48Z37nRm5w-_1bPylh1tThoCAa0QAvD_BwE.

BIBLIOGRAPHY

REFERENCES FOR CHAPTER 4
References for Chapter 4 Epigraphs
Chicago Public Schools.—quoted by Cheung, A. (2015, April 29). Use of restrooms, locker rooms by transgender students outlined by CPS. Dnainfo.com. Retrieved from: https://www.dnainfo.com/chicago/20150429/boystown/use-of-restrooms-locker-rooms-by-transgender-students-outlined-by-cps.

Chicago Public Schools.—quoted by Migdon, B. (2021, December 7). Gender neutral restroom signs posted at Chicago public schools. Thehill.com. Retrieved from: https://thehill.com/changing-america/enrichment/education/584806-gender-neutral-restroom-signs-posted-at-chicago-public.

Little, D.—quoted by Swartz, T. (2021, December 14). CPS says new "boys+" and "girls+" bathroom signs are gender inclusive; petition seeks to rescind policy. *Chicago Tribune.* Retrieved from: https://www.chicagotribune.com/news/breaking/ct-chicago-public-schools-bathroom-policy-gender-20211214-shb3sqqgt5gxdbukqyxnypulem-story.html.

Migdon, B. (2021, December 7). Gender neutral restroom signs posted at Chicago public schools. Thehill.com. Retrieved from: https://thehill.com/changing-america/enrichment/education/584806-gender-neutral-restroom-signs-posted-at-chicago-public.

Russell, N. (2021, December 6). Chicago Public Schools' new "gender equity" restroom policy ignores biology, invades students' privacy. Dailysignal.com. Retrieved from: https://www.dailysignal.com/2021/12/06/chicago-public-schools-new-gender-equity-restroom-policy-ignores-biology-invades-students-privacy.

Unidentified Chicago Parent.—quoted by Migdon, B. (2021, December 7). Gender neutral restroom signs posted at Chicago public schools. Thehill.com. Retrieved from: https://thehill.com/changing-america/enrichment/education/584806-gender-neutral-restroom-signs-posted-at-chicago-public.

References for Easing Passenger Anxiety on Flights—Introduction
Alt, K. (2022, March 25). Service dog vs therapy dog vs emotional support dogs. Caninejournal.com. Retrieved from: https://www.caninejournal.com/service-dog-vs-therapy-dog-vs-emotional-support-dogs.

Delta Air Lines Advertiser Profile. (2022). Mediaradar.com. Retrieved from: https://advertisers.mediaradar.com/delta-air-lines-advertising-profile#:~:text=Summary,year%20across%20multiple%20Media%20formats.

Delta Air Lines Inc.'s operating revenue from FY 2008 to FY 2021. (2022, February). Statista.com. Retrieved from: https://www.statista.com/statistics/220809/operating-revenue-of-delta-air-lines.

Delta Air Lines Revenue 2010–2021 (2022). Macrotrends.net. Retrieved from: https://www.macrotrends.net/stocks/charts/DAL/delta-air-lines/revenue

Delta Awards & Recognition. (2022). Delta.com. Retrieved from: https://news.delta.com/category/awards-recognition.

Gibeault, S. (2021, February 24). Everything you need to know about emotional support animals. Akc.org. Retrieved from: https://www.akc.org/expert-advice/news/everything-about-emotional-support-animals.

Rains, T. (2021, November 25). See how pets are transported on commercial airlines as animals increasingly accompany customers on vacation. Businessinsider.com. Retrieved from: https://www.businessinsider.com/how-your-pets-are-transported-on-commercial-airlines-2021-10.

Reisen, J. (2021, February 24). Service dogs, working dogs, therapy dogs, emotional support dogs: What's the difference? Akc.org. Retrieved from: https://www.akc.org/expert-advice/training/service-working-therapy-emotional-support-dogs.

U.S. Department of Justice. (2015). Frequently asked questions about service animals and the ADA. Retrieved from: https://www.ada.gov/regs2010/service_animal_qa.html.

U.S. Department of Transportation. (2020, December 2). U.S. Department of Transportation announces final rule on traveling by air with service animals. Retrieved from: https://www.transportation.gov/briefing-room/us-department-transportation-announces-final-rule-traveling-air-service-animals.

Wall Street Journal. (2022) Why man's best friend may be man's best co-worker. Retrieved from: https://partners.wsj.com/cesar/not-just-something-to-wag-about/why-mans-best-friend-may-be-mans-best-co-worker.

Yamanouchi, K. (2020, January 14). Delta reports $47 billion in revenue in record year. *Atlanta Journal-Constitution.* Retrieved from: https://www.ajc.com/business/delta-reports-billion-revenue-record-year/jWx2unvuSWuc2f7a07KXMJ.

References for Easing Passenger Anxiety on Flights—Enthusiasts

Abramson, A. (2020, February 11). Coronavirus threat escalates fears—and bigotry. American Psychological Association. Retrieved from: https://www.apa.org/news/apa/2020/coronavirus-threat.

Apibhs.com. (2020, May 18). How emotional support animals benefit mental health and wellness. [Blog]. Retrieved from: https://apibhs.com/2020/05/18/how-emotional-support-animals-benefit-mental-health-and-wellness.

Cleveland Clinic. (2021, February 1). Illness Anxiety Disorder [Hypochondria, Hypochondriasis]. Retrieved from: https://my.clevelandclinic.org/health/diseases/9886-illness-anxiety-disorder-hypochondria-hypochondriasis.

Conlon, P. (2021, September 21). Psychiatric service dog. Certapet.com. Retrieved from: https://www.certapet.com/psychiatric-service-dog.

Donaldson, S. (2022, March 17). With emotional-support animals on the rise, how are colleges responding? *Chronicle of Higher Education.* Retrieved from: https://www.chronicle.com/article/with-emotional-support-animals-on-the-rise-how-are-colleges-responding.

Fischhoff, B. (2020, February). Speaking of psychology: Coronavirus anxiety. American Psychological Association. Retrieved from: https://www.apa.org/news/podcasts/speaking-of-psychology/coronavirus-anxiety.

Singh, R. J. (2022, January 13). Delta Air sees a fast recovery from Omicron turbulence. Reuters.com. Retrieved from: https://www.reuters.com/business/aerospace

Bibliography

-defense/delta-air-warns-loss-current-quarter-after-stronger-than-expected-q4-profit-2022-01-13.

References for Easing Passenger Anxiety on Flights—Skeptics

Atwood, S. (2022, October 16). Influx of emotional support animals prompts Michigan legislation. *Detroit News*. Retrieved from: https://www.detroitnews.com/story/news/local/michigan/2022/10/16/influx-of-emotional-support-animals-fake-certificates-prompts-michigan-legislation/69565194007.

Kime, P. (2021, August 4). New rules barring emotional support animals on patriot express flights send military families scrambling. Military.com. Retrieved from: https://www.military.com/daily-news/2021/08/04/new-rules-barring-emotional-support-animals-patriot-express-flights-send-military-families.html.

LAMag.com. (2021, August 6). Best emotional support animal letter services: Top 3 sites to use at home. (2021, August 6). Lamag.com. Retrieved from: https://www.lamag.com/article/best-emotional-support-animal-letter-services-top-3-sites-to-use-at-home.

References for Easing Student Anxiety in Restrooms—Introduction

Gattupalli, A. (2022, June 28). Designing around debate: The gender-neutral bathroom. Archdaily.com. Retrieved from: https://www.archdaily.com/984280/designing-around-debate-the-gender-neutral-bathroom.

Gender inclusive schools. (2022). Restrooms and facilities. Genderinclusiveschools.org. Retrieved from: https://www.genderinclusiveschools.org/restrooms-transgender-student-policy.

OpIndia.com. (2021, December 3). All public schools in Chicago go "woke," gender-neutral toilets made mandatory for students. Retrieved from: https://www.opindia.com/2021/12/all-schools-chicago-usa-go-woke-gender-neutral-toilets-made-mandatory.

References for Easing Student Anxiety in Restrooms—Enthusiasts

Kralik, J. (July 2016). School bathroom access for transgender students. Ncsl.org. Retrieved from: https://www.ncsl.org/research/education/school-bathroom-access-for-transgender-students.aspx.

Pinsker, J. (2019, January 23). The long lines for women's bathrooms could be eliminated. Why haven't they been? *The Atlantic*. Retrieved from: https://www.theatlantic.com/family/archive/2019/01/women-men-bathroom-lines-wait/580993.

Saunders, J. (2022, January 20). Justice Dept. will argue for transgender student. *Florida Times-Union*. Retrieved from: https://www.jacksonville.com/story/news/courts/2022/01/20/feds-argue-transgender-student-st-johns-bathroom-case/6595964001.

Swartz, T. (2021, December 14). CPS says new "boys+" and "girls+" bathroom signs are gender inclusive; petition seeks to rescind policy. *Chicago Tribune*. Retrieved

from: https://www.chicagotribune.com/news/breaking/ct-chicago-public-schools-bathroom-policy-gender-20211214-shb3sqqgt5gxdbukqyxnypulem-story.html.
- Wernz, J. (2021, December 19). Are "Gender Plus" bathrooms new: And how should schools handle them? Titleixtips.com. Retrieved from: https://titleixtips.com/are-gender-plus-bathrooms-new-and-how-should-schools-handle-them.

References for Easing Student Anxiety in Restrooms—Skeptics
- Davis, M., Heffernan, M., Smith, T., Bendelow, A., & Bhatti, P. (2019, December 2). Chicago parents identify the top 10 social issues affecting youth 2018–19. Luriechildrens.org. Retrieved from: https://www.luriechildrens.org/en/voices-of-child-health-in-chicago/chicago-parents-identify-the-top-10-social-issues-affecting-youth-2018-19.
- Graham, A. (2021, April 15). Hundreds show up to speak on Lee Schools' bathroom policy for transgender students. Nbc-2.com. Retrieved from: https://nbc-2.com/news/local/2021/04/14/misinformation-over-lee-schools-bathroom-policy-causes-public-outrage.
- McCabe, P. (2021, April 14). Lee school board LGBTQ flyer in Code of Conduct draws crowd of hundreds. *Fort Myers News-Press*. Retrieved from: https://www.news-press.com/story/news/education/2021/04/14/lee-school-board-lgbtq-flyer-code-conduct-draws-critics/7214547002.
- Newberry, L. (2022, March 7). Why gender-neutral bathrooms benefit all young people. *Los Angeles Times*. Retrieved from: https://www.latimes.com/california/newsletter/2022-03-07/8-to-3-template-8-to-3.
- Whitney, B. (2021, September 16). Tensions run high at high school over gender-neutral bathrooms. Kesq.com. Retrieved from: https://kesq.com/cnn-regional/2021/09/16/tensions-run-high-at-high-school-over-gender-neutral-bathrooms/.

REFERENCES FOR CHAPTER 5
References for Chapter 5 Epigraphs
- Anti-Defamation League. (2017, May 12). Unconstitutional backdoor school prayer bill will have unintended consequences. Retrieved from: https://www.adl.org/blog/unconstitutional-backdoor-school-prayer-bill-will-have-unintended-consequences.
- Berman, L.—quoted by Gaffney, R. (2021, June 14). DeSantis signs bill requiring moments of silence in K-12 schools. Wfsu.org. Retrieved from: https://news.wfsu.org/state-news/2021-06-14/desantis-signs-bill-requiring-moments-of-silence-in-k-12-schools.
- Dailey, R. (2021, June 14). DeSantis signs bill to require daily school moment of silence. News4jax.com. Retrieved from: https://www.news4jax.com/news/local/2021/06/14/desantis-signs-bill-to-require-daily-school-moment-of-silence.
- DeSantis, R.—quoted by Duster, C. & Lynch, J. (2021, June 15). Florida governor signs new bill requiring K-12 public schools to hold moment of silence each

day. Cnn.com. Retrieved from: https://www.cnn.com/2021/06/15/politics/florida-public-schools-moment-of-silence/index.html.
Hanna, R.—quoted by Smalls, T. (2021, September 16). New "moment of silence" law alters public schools. Thefamuanonline.com. Retrieved from: http://www.thefamuanonline.com/2021/09/16/tashai-smalls-staff-writer.
Kilbride, L. (2017, June 21). Florida religious expression in schools legislation now law. Wjct.org. Retrieved from: https://news.wjct.org/education/2017-06-21/florida-religious-expression-in-schools-legislation-now-law.
Pizzo, J.—quoted by Caina, B. C. (2021, June 14). Florida Governor signs bill requiring moment for school prayer. Nbcmiami.com. Retrieved from: https://www.nbcmiami.com/news/local/florida-governor-signs-bill-requiring-school-moments-of-silence/2472296.
Van Zant, C.—quoted by Larrabee, B. (2012, March 23). Scott signs school "prayer" bill; Opponents warn of legal challenges. Jacksonville.com. Retrieved from: https://www.jacksonville.com/story/news/politics/2012/03/23/scott-signs-school-prayer-bill-opponents-warn-legal-challenges/15871908007.

References for Fostering Voter Deliberation—Introduction

Frimodig, B. (2022, March 28). What are heuristics? Simplypsychology.org. Retrieved from: www.simplypsychology.org/what-is-a-heuristic.html.
Montanaro, D. (2021, June 23). Ranked-choice voting gets a prime-time shot under New York city's bright lights. Npr.org. Retrieved from: https://www.npr.org/2021/06/22/1008807504/ranked-choice-voting-new-york-city-mayors-race.
Prokopandrew, A. (2021, July 8). New York City's mayoral primary is over. Vox.com. Retrieved from: https://www.vox.com/22565095/ranked-choice-adams-garcia-wiley-nyc.
Ruhl, C. (2021, May 4). What is cognitive bias? Simplypsychology.org. Retrieved from: https://www.simplypsychology.org/cognitive-bias.html#:~:text=A%20cognitive%20bias%20is%20a,making%20quicker%20and%20more%20efficient.

References for Fostering Voter Deliberation—Enthusiasts

Almukhtar, S., Hughes, J., & Weingart, E. (2021, April 22). How does ranked-choice voting work in New York? *New York Times*. Retrieved from: https://www.nytimes.com/interactive/2021/nyregion/ranked-choice-voting-nyc.html.
Fuchs, E. R. (2021, May 27). What is ranked-choice voting and why is New York City using it? News.columbia.edu. Retrieved from: https://news.columbia.edu/news/ranked-choice-voting-nyc.
Kambhampaty, A. P. (2019, November 6). New York City voters just adopted ranked-choice voting in elections: Here's how it works. *Time*. Retrieved from: https://time.com/5718941/ranked-choice-voting.
New York City Government. (2022). Ranked choice voting. Author. Retrieved from: https://www1.nyc.gov/site/civicengagement/voting/ranked-choice-voting.page.

Ruiz, R., Gómez, J., & Corse, A. (2021, June 22). What is ranked choice voting? NYC's ballot explained, with bagels. *Wall Street Journal*. Retrieved from: https://www.wsj.com/articles/confused-by-nycs-ranked-choice-mayoral-primary-practice-with-bagels-11622631601.

References for Fostering Voter Deliberation—Skeptics

Wall Street Journal Editorial Board. (2021, June 30). New York's ranked-choice fiasco. *Wall Street Journal*. Retrieved from: https://www.wsj.com/articles/new-yorks-ranked-choice-fiasco-11625092570.

Weber, V., & Meeks, A. (2021, July 9). Ranked-choice voting helped wreck Minneapolis. *Wall Street Journal*. Retrieved from: https://www.wsj.com/articles/ranked-choice-voting-helped-wreck-minneapolis-11625854937?mod=trending_now_opn_4.

References for Fostering Student Deliberation—Introduction

Abdill, R. (2012, February 6). Five Supreme Court cases that say Florida's prayer in schools bill is bunk. Browardpalmbeach.com. Retrieved from: https://www.browardpalmbeach.com/news/five-supreme-court-cases-that-say-floridas-prayer-in-schools-bill-is-bunk-6449955.

Bravin, J. (2022b, April 25). Supreme Court mulls impact of high school coach's 50-yard-line prayers. *Wall Street Journal*. Retrieved from: https://www.wsj.com/articles/supreme-court-mulls-impact-of-high-school-coachs-50-yard-line-prayers-11650918003?mod=hp_listc_pos3.

Giordano, G. (2009). *Solving education's problems effectively: A guide to using the case method*. Lanham, MD: Rowman & Littlefield Education.

Giordano, G. (2019). *Parents and textbooks: Answers that reveal essential steps for improvement*. Lanham, MD: Rowman & Littlefield Education.

Jones, S. P., & Sheffield, E. C. (Eds.). (2009). *The role of religion in 21st-century public schools*. New York: P. Lang.

Laats, A. (2015). *The other school reformers: Conservative activism in American education*. Cambridge, MA: Harvard University Press.

Russo, C. J. (2013). *Religion in schools*. Thousand Oaks, CA: Sage.

WPBF.com (2022, June 15). Florida schools to require "moment of silence" every day. Retrieved from: https://www.wpbf.com/article/florida-governor-ron-desantis-surfside-plane-rerouted/36717000#.

References for Fostering Student Deliberation—Enthusiasts

Bravin, J. (2022a, April 24). High-school football coach takes case for prayer to supreme court. *Wall Street Journal*. Retrieved from: https://www.wsj.com/articles/high-school-football-coach-takes-case-for-prayer-to-supreme-court-11650798000?mod=hp_lead_pos10.

Justice, B., & Macleod, C. M. (2016). *Have a little faith: Religion, democracy, and the American public school*. Chicago: The University of Chicago Press.

Thomas, R. M. (2008). *God in the classroom: Religion and America's public schools.* Lanham, MD: Rowman & Littlefield.

References for Fostering Student Deliberation—Skeptics
Bloch, E. (2021a, October 7). Bible event promoted by public school, sparking concern. *Florida Times—Union.* Retrieved from: https://jacksonville-fl-app.newsmemory.com/?publink=3a5459aff_1345f63.

Bloch, E. (2021b, October 10). Terry Parker High promotes prayer event on campus, raising concerns. *Florida Times—Union.* Retrieved from: https://jacksonville-fl-app.newsmemory.com/?publink=3669a40cc_1345f66.

Duster, C., & Lynch, J. (2021, June 15). Florida governor signs new bill requiring K-12 public schools to hold moment of silence each day. Cnn.com. Retrieved from: https://www.cnn.com/2021/06/15/politics/florida-public-schools-moment-of-silence/index.html.

Esposito, J. L., & Kalin, I. (Eds.). (2011). *Islamophobia: The challenge of pluralism in the 21st century.* New York: Oxford University Press.

Mitchell, S. A., & Quli, N. E. (Eds.). (2015). *Buddhism beyond borders: New perspectives on Buddhism in the United States.* Albany: State University of New York Press.

REFERENCES FOR CHAPTER 6
References for Chapter 6 Epigraphs
Borges, S., & Mitchell, R. S. (2018). *Give me shelter: Architecture takes on the homeless crisis.* Novato, CA: Oro.

Carvalho, A.—quoted in Vlachou, M. (2022, August 11). LA City Council votes to outlaw homeless camps near schools, day care centers. *Huffington Post.* Retrieved from: https://www.huffpost.com/entry/la-city-council-homeless-camps-school-ban_n_62f4dee9e4b0288b61a1f8c9.

City News Service. (2022, July 1). LA City Council votes to ban homeless encampments near schools. Patch.com. Retrieved from: https://patch.com/california/los-angeles/la-city-council-votes-ban-homeless-encampments-near-schools.

Committee for Greater LA. (2022). We're not giving up: A plan for homelessness governance in Los Angeles. Retrieved from: https://nogoingback.la/action-teams/homelessness.

Garcetti, E.—quoted by Garcetti, E., & Martin, M. (2019, September 21). LA Mayor Eric Garcetti calls homelessness the "humanitarian crisis of our lives." Npr.org. Retrieved from: https://www.npr.org/2019/09/21/763073646/l-a-mayor-eric-garcetti-calls-homelessness-the-humanitarian-crisis-of-our-lives.

Koretz, P.—quoted by Richard, L. (2022, August 10). Protesters disrupt Los Angeles City Council vote on banning homeless encampments near schools. Foxnews.com. Retrieved from: https://www.foxnews.com/us/protesters-disrupt-los-angeles-city-council-vote-banning-homeless-encampments-near-schools.

Shure, N. (2021, August 3). Los Angeles liberals' brutal campaign against the homeless. *New Republic.* Retrieved from: https://newrepublic.com/article/163141/los-angeles-homeless-garcetti-katzenberg.

Unnamed Los Angeles School Principal.—quoted in LA City Council votes to ban homeless encampments near schools. (2022, July 1). Foxla.com. Retrieved from: https://www.foxla.com/news/los-angeles-homeless-encampments-near-schools.

References for Marketing Analytics—Introduction

Gillan, J. (2011). *Television and new media: Must-click TV.* New York: Routledge.

PPCexpo.com. (2022). Examples of marketing analytics: Real-life challenges while doing analysis in PPC. Retrieved from: https://ppcexpo.com/blog/examples-of-marketing-analytics.

Putler, D., & Krider, R. (2015). *Customer and business analytics.* Boca Raton, FL: CRC Press.

Rodrigues, J. (2021). *Product analytics: Applied data science techniques for actionable consumer insights.* Boston: Addison-Wesley.

References for Marketing Analytics—Enthusiasts

Sanders, C. S., & Weissman, G. (1987). *Champagne Music: The Lawrence Welk Show.* New York: St. Martin's Press.

References for Marketing Analytics—Skeptics

Buzzard, K. (2012). *Tracking the audience: The ratings industry from analog to digital.* New York: Routledge.

Clarendon, D. (2021, July 28). Why have TV networks turned against Nielsen ratings? Tvinsider.com. Retrieved from: https://www.tvinsider.com/1006916/tv-network-nielsen-ratings-vab-mrc-accreditation.

Lawrence Welk. (2019). Spaceagepop.com. Retrieved from: http://www.spaceagepop.com/welk.htm.

Porter, R. (2021, September 8). Nielsen under siege: Who (if anyone) will capitalize on the ratings giant's woes? Hollywoodreporter.com. Retrieved from: https://www.hollywoodreporter.com/business/business-news/nielsen-woes-tv-ratings-1235009554-1235009554.

References for Campaign Analytics—Introduction

Barnes, K. (2022, February 22). 51,000 homeless students are in LA public schools: How are they getting help? Kcrw.com. Retrieved from: https://www.kcrw.com/news/shows/greater-la/homeless-bikes-oc/la-public-schools-unhoused-students.

Denton, R. E., Trent, J. S., & Friedenberg, R. V. (2020). *Political campaign communication: Principles and practices.* Lanham, MD: Rowman & Littlefield.

National Center for Homeless Education. (2021). Student homelessness in America. Author. Retrieved from: https://nche.ed.gov.

Resonate.com. (2022). Win the battle for hearts and minds with hyper-relevant data. . Retrieved from: https://insights.resonate.com/pa-overview.

Swaak, T. (2018, November 28). LAUSD board approves study of housing homeless students and their families on district properties. Laschoolreport.com. Retrieved from: https://www.laschoolreport.com/lausd-board-approves-study-of-housing-homeless-students-and-their-families-on-district-properties.

Swain, E. (2020, November 6). Homeless student figures exceed 269,000 in California. Invisiblepeople.tv. Retrieved from: https://invisiblepeople.tv/homeless-student-figures-rise-past-269000-in-california/.

Tickamyer, A. R., Sherman, J., & Warlick, J. L. (Eds.). (2017). *Rural poverty in the United States*. New York: Columbia University Press.

Tower, C. C., & White, D. J.(1989). *Homeless students*. Washington, DC. National Education Association.

References for Campaign Analytics—Enthusiasts

Los Angeles County Office of Education. (2022). Homeless children and youth. Retrieved from: https://www.lacoe.edu/Student-Services/Homeless-Children-Youth.

Los Angeles Homeless Services Authority. (2021, June 3). LAHSA provides 2020 update on youth homelessness. Retrieved from: https://www.lahsa.org/news?article=750-lahsa-provides-2020-update-on-youth-homelessness.

Los Angeles Unified School District. (2022). Homeless Education Office. Retrieved from: https://achieve.lausd.net/Page/12911.

Schoolhouseconnection.com. (2021, March 10). Congress passes the *American Rescue Act Plan*: Funding for homeless children and youth included. Retrieved from: https://schoolhouseconnection.org/congress-passes-the-american-rescue-act-plan-funding-for-homeless-children-and-youth-included.

Schoolhouseconnection.com. (2021, September 22). Five facts educators need to know about student homelessness—and actions to take. Retrieved from: https://schoolhouseconnection.org/five-facts-educators-need-to-know-about-student-homelessness/#:~:text=Both%20the%20American%20Rescue%20Plan,children%20and%20youth%20experiencing%20homelessness%2C.

Strauss, L. (2022, October 21). My colleague was stabbed. Homelessness and peril are much closer to home than you think. *USA TODAY*. Retrieved from: https://www.usatoday.com/story/opinion/contributors/2022/10/21/homelessness-crisis-america-result-collective-indifference/10533060002.

References for Campaign Analytics—Skeptics

Chen, G. (2022, May 19). 10 challenges for the Los Angeles Unified School District. Publicschoolreview.com. Retrieved from: https://www.publicschoolreview.com/blog/10-challenges-for-the-los-angeles-unified-school-district.

Chua, L. (2022, February 23). LA is paying $600,000 apiece for units to house homeless people. Bloomberg.com. Retrieved from: https://www.bloomberg.com/news

/articles/2022-02-23/la-paying-600-000-apiece-for-units-to-house-homeless-people.

Lauterbach, C. (2021, June 2). Poll: California parents sour on public schools after pandemic. Thecentersquare.com. Retrieved from: https://www.thecentersquare.com/california/poll-california-parents-souron-public-schools-after-pandemic/article_d7362418-c3d7-11eb-b808-5b.

Kane, T. (2022, May). Kids are far, far behind in school. *The Atlantic*. Retrieved from: https://www.theatlantic.com/ideas/archive/2022/05/schools-learning-loss-remote-covid-education/629938.

McGinniss, J. (1968). *The selling of the president*. New York: Trident.

NBCNews.com. (2019, January 15). Some Los Angeles parents support the teachers' strike despite challenges it brings. Retrieved from: https://www.nbcnews.com/news/us-news/some-los-angeles-parents-support-teachers-strike-despite-challenges-it-n959116.

Sand, L. (2021, November 30). Parents "don't get how teaching works." Californiapolicycenter.org. Retrieved from: https://californiapolicycenter.org/parents-dont-get-how-teaching-works.

References for Chapter 7
References for Chapter 7 Epigraphs

Anonymous Parent.—quoted by Levesque, B. (2021, September 20). Students hurl anti-LGBTQ slurs at GSA kids in St. John's County Florida. Losangelesblade.com. Retrieved from: https://www.losangelesblade.com/2021/09/20/students-hurl-anti-lgbtq-slurs-at-gsa-kids-in-st-johns-county-florida.

Anonymous Teacher.—quoted by Hobbs, K. (2022, February 9). St. Johns teachers fear they must "out" LGBTQ students to parents. Wjct.org. Retrieved from: https://news.wjct.org/first-coast/2022-02-09/teachers-alarmed-by-lgbtq-policy-in-st-johns-schools.

Hill-Nobles, C.—quoted by McLean, J. (2022, February 11). Advocates share concerns over SJC school district's "guidelines for LGBTQ+ students." News4jax.com. Retrieved from: https://www.news4jax.com/news/local/2022/02/11/advocates-share-concerns-over-sjc-school-districts-guidelines-for-lgbtq-students.

Midyette, J.—quoted by Schindler, A. (2022, February 9). Teachers must tell parents before using a student's preferred name or gender pronouns in St. Johns County Schools. Firstcoastnews.com. Retrieved from: https://www.firstcoastnews.com/article/news/education/teachers-must-tell-parents-before-using-students-preferred-name-gender-pronouns-st-johns-county-schools/77-daf6b06b-8539-4e59-b91d-c5f547d9fcff.

Perez, W.—quoted by Tracy, K. (2022, January 27). Lawsuit claims Clay County Schools withheld information about child's well-being before student attempted suicide. Firstcoastnews.com. Retrieved from: https://www.firstcoastnews.com/article/news/education/parents-file-lawsuit-against-clay-county-schools-say-administrators-didnt-disclose-meetings-about-gender-identity-confusion-district-denies-claims/77-e2a135bd-ef65-4c35-999e-6b39ece496dd.

St. Johns County Schools. (2021). Best practices LGBTQ 2021. Retrieved from: https://www.scribd.com/document/557874328/St-Johns-County-Schools-Best-Practices-LGBTQ-2021.

References for Film Disclosures—Introduction

Anderton, C. (2015, March 12). Auto-Tune: The controversy that will not die. Mixonline.com. Retrieved from: https://www.mixonline.com/blog/auto-tune-the-controversy-that-will-not-die.

Etienne, V. (2021, July 19). What to know about the controversy surrounding Anthony Bourdain's A.I. Voice used in Roadrunner. People.com. Retrieved from: https://people.com/food/what-to-know-about-anthony-bourdains-a-i-voice-controversy-in-new-doc-roadrunner.

Gopani, A. (2021, July 22). The curious case of Anthony Bourdain's AI voice. Analyticsindiamag.com. Retrieved from: https://analyticsindiamag.com/the-curious-case-of-anthony-bourdains-ai-voice.

Hughes, D. (2015, May-June). Technological pitch correction: Controversy, contexts, and considerations. *Journal of Singing*. Retrieved from: https://go.gale.com/ps/i.do?p=AONE&u=googlescholar&id=GALE|A414840803&v=2.1&it=r&sid=googleScholar&asid=71c7d810.

Perez, J. (2022). Pro tools guide: How to use AutoTune & pitch correction? Integraudio.com. Retrieved from: https://integraudio.com/pro-tools-guide-how-to-autotune.

Prisco, J., & Stewart, A. (2015, May 27). The invention that changed music forever. Cnn.com. Retrieved from: https://www.cnn.com/2015/05/26/tech/autotune-inventor-mci/index.html.

Rice, Q. C. (2021, July 17). The ethics of voice cloning. https://www.claytonrice.com/the-ethics-of-voice-cloning.

Rise of ethical voice cloning in the deepfake voice wars. (2022, April 12). Respeecher.com. Retrieved from: https://www.respeecher.com/blog/the-rise-of-ethical-voice-cloning-in-the-deepfake-voice-wars.

Salia, R. (2021, March 26). Top 10 best deepfake voice software review. Retrieved from: https://topten.ai/best-deepfake-voice-tools-review.

Waugh. R. (2021, October 19). How Cher's producers tried to keep her famous "Believe" Auto-Tune secret. Uk.news.yahoo.com. Retrieved from: https://uk.news.yahoo.com/cher-believe-autotune-061938631.html.

Wellsaidlabs.com. (2022). Convert text to voice in real time. Retrieved from: https://wellsaidlabs.com.

References for Film Disclosures—Enthusiasts

Bentley, J. (2021, September 29). "Roadrunner" director Morgan Neville on Anthony Bourdain AI controversy: "I stand by it." Indiewire.com. Retrieved from: https://www.indiewire.com/video/anthony-bourdain-doc-director-on-ai-controversy-1234668118.

Gerber, D. (2021, July 16). A.I. voice of Anthony Bourdain in new "Roadrunner" documentary sparks controversy. *Boston Globe*. Retrieved from: https://www.bostonglobe.com/2021/07/16/arts/ai-voice-anthony-bourdain-new-roadrunner-documentary-sparks-controversy.

O'Neill, J. (2021, July 15). Anthony Bourdain doc director admits to using A.I. to fake voice. *New York Post*. Retrieved from: https://nypost.com/2021/07/15/director-of-anthony-bourdain-admits-to-using-a-i-voice-over.

Pearce, M. (2021, July 15). AI deepfakes of Anthony Bourdain's voice are only a taste of what's coming. *Los Angeles Times*. Retrieved from: https://www.latimes.com/entertainment-arts/story/2021-07-26/la-et-anthony-bourdain-deepfake-ai-voice-documentary-audio-cgi.

References for Film Disclosures—Skeptics

Abouther.com. (2021). Anthony Bourdain's voice cloning is scary & here's why. Retrieved from: https://www.abouther.com/node/40541/entertainment/music-film-television/anthony-bourdains-voice-cloning-scary-heres-why.

BBC.com. (2021, July 16). AI narration of chef Anthony Bourdain's voice sparks row. Retrieved from: https://www.bbc.com/news/technology-57842514.

Gershgorn, D. (2021, July 15). New Anthony Bourdain documentary deepfakes his voice. Theverge.com. Retrieved from: https://www.theverge.com/2021/7/15/22578707/anthony-bourdain-documentary-deepfake-voice.

Herman, A. (2021, July 20). The double-edged ethics of the Anthony Bourdain documentary "Roadrunner." Theringer.com. Retrieved from: https://www.theringer.com/movies/2021/7/20/22584986/anthony-bourdain-roadrunner-documentary-movie-ethics.

Hornaday, A. (2021, July 19). The controversy over Anthony Bourdain's deepfaked voice is a reminder that documentaries aren't journalism. *Washington Post*. Retrieved from: https://www.washingtonpost.com/entertainment/anthony-bourdain-roadrunner-deepfake-documentaries/2021/07/19/9b582702-e7c7-11eb-97a0-a09d10181e36_story.html.

Kreps, D. (2021, July 16). Anthony Bourdain's widow denies she authorized controversial ai voiceover in "Roadrunner." *Rolling Stone*. Retrieved from: https://www.rollingstone.com/tv-movies/tv-movie-news/anthony-bourdain-widow-ai-voiceover-roadrunner-1198374.

Maravegias, J. (2021, July 16). Controversies over Anthony Bourdain documentary hurt the women he loved. Pajiba.com. Retrieved from: https://www.pajiba.com/film_reviews/controversies-over-anthony-bourdain-documentary-hurt-the-women-he-loved.php.

Murray, N. (2021, Aaugust 23). The Roadrunner deepfake voice controversy and ethics in AI. Readspeaker.ai/blog. Retrieved from: https://www.readspeaker.ai/blog/deepfake-voice.

O'Brien, M., & Ortutay, B. (2021, July 16). Why the Anthony Bourdain voice cloning in documentary "Roadrunner" creeps people out. *USA TODAY*. Retrieved from: https:

//www.usatoday.com/story/entertainment/movies/2021/07/16/anthony-bourdain-voice-cloning-artificial-intelligence/8000861002.

Rosner, H. (2021, July 17). The ethics of a deepfake Anthony Bourdain voice. *New Yorker*. Retrieved from: https://www.newyorker.com/culture/annals-of-gastronomy/the-ethics-of-a-deepfake-anthony-bourdain-voice.

References for Student Disclosures—Introduction

Creitz, C. (2021, November 17). Loudoun, Virginia teacher speaks out after court win over transgenderism critique. Foxnews.com. Retrieved from: https://www.foxnews.com/media/loudoun-virginia-teacher-speaks-out-after-court-win-over-transgenderism-critique.

Jones, Z. C. (2021, November 19). Parents sue Wisconsin school district over gender identity policy. Cbsnews.com. Retrieved from: https://www.cbsnews.com/news/gender-pronoun-wisconsin-kettle-moraine-school-lawsuit-transition.

Migdon, B. (2022, July 8). A Wisconsin school district policy preventing staff from outing trans students will stay in effect for now, court rules. Thehill.com. Retrieved from: https://thehill.com/changing-america/respect/equality/3550244-a-wisconsin-school-district-policy-preventing-staff-from-outing-trans-students-will-stay-in-effect-for-now-court-rules.

Minock, N. (2022, June 29). Lawsuit filed against Loudoun Co. schools for allegedly violating parental rights. Wjla.com. Retrieved from: https://wjla.com/news/local/loudoun-county-superintendent-scott-ziegler-schools-lawsuit-filed-board-sex-assault-gender-transitions-pornographic-books-misconduct-public-education-parents-students-children-lcps-afl-parent-rights.

Yancey-Bragg, N. (2021, July 13). School district fights court's decision to reinstate teacher. *USA TODAY*. Retrieved from: https://www.usatoday.com/story/news/education/2021/07/12/virginia-school-district-appeals-judge-decision-reinstate-teacher-tanner-cross/7935546002.

References for Student Disclosures—Enthusiasts

Jones, A. (2022, March 28). Teachers speak out against Florida's "Parental Rights in Education" bill. Cbsnews.com. Retrieved from: https://www.cbsnews.com/news/teachers-florida-parental-rights-in-education-dont-say-gay-bill.

Levesque, B. (2021 September 20). Students hurl anti-LGBTQ slurs at GSA kids in St. John's County Florida. Losangelesblade.com. Retrieved from: https://www.losangelesblade.com/2021/09/20/students-hurl-anti-lgbtq-slurs-at-gsa-kids-in-st-johns-county-florida.

McLean, J. (2022, February 11). Advocates share concerns over SJC school district's "guidelines for LGBTQ+ students." News4jax.com. Retrieved from: https://www.news4jax.com/news/local/2022/02/11/advocates-share-concerns-over-sjc-school-districts-guidelines-for-lgbtq-students.

NPR.org. (2022, April 5). What Florida's Parental Rights in Education Law means for teachers. Retrieved from: https://www.npr.org/2022/04/04/1090946670/what-floridas-parental-rights-in-education-law-means-for-teachers.

References for Student Disclosures—Skeptics

Chasmar, J. (2022, March 28). Florida's DeSantis signs Parental Rights in Education bill, hits back at Hollywood critics. Retrieved from: Foxnews.com. https://www.foxnews.com/politics/florida-desantis-signs-parental-rights-education-bill.

First Coast News. (2022, July 11). Duval School Board votes 7–0 to change services in compliance with Parental Rights in Education law. Retrieved from: https://www.firstcoastnews.com/article/news/education/duval-county-school-board-vote-on-parental-rights-education-law/77-1baf2db7-4e03-4513-b1a2-a7daa64bcf79.

Florida House of Representatives. (2021, July 1). HB 241—Parents' Bill of Rights. Author. Retrieved from: https://www.flsenate.gov/Committees/billsummaries/2021/html/2475.

Florida House of Representatives. (2022, July 1). CS/CS/HB 1557—Parental Rights in Education. Retrieved from: https://www.myfloridahouse.gov/Sections/Bills/billsdetail.aspx?BillId=76745.

Hobbs, K. (2022, February 9). St. Johns teachers fear they must "out" LGBTQ students to parents. Wjct.org. Retrieved from: https://news.wjct.org/first-coast/2022-02-09/teachers-alarmed-by-lgbtq-policy-in-st-johns-schools.

Ogles, J. (2021, June 30). Parents' Bill of Rights signed into law in Florida. Floridapolitics.com. Retrieved from: https://floridapolitics.com/archives/438620-parents-bill-of-rights-signed-into-law-in-florida.

Schindler, A. (2022, February 9). Teachers must tell parents before using a student's preferred name or gender pronouns in St. Johns County Schools. Firstcoastnews.com. Retrieved from: https://www.firstcoastnews.com/article/news/education/teachers-must-tell-parents-before-using-students-preferred-name-gender-pronouns-st-johns-county-schools/77-daf6b06b-8539-4e59-b91d-c5f547d9fcff.

Tracy, K. (2022, January 27). Lawsuit claims Clay County Schools withheld information about child's well-being before student attempted suicide. Firstcoastnews.com. Retrieved from: https://www.firstcoastnews.com/article/news/education/parents-file-lawsuit-against-clay-county-schools-say-administrators-didnt-disclose-meetings-about-gender-identity-confusion-district-denies-claims/77-e2a135bd-ef65-4c35-999e-6b39ece496dd.

REFERENCES FOR CHAPTER 8

References for Chapter 8 Epigraphs

California Proposition 227. (1998, June 2). English language in public schools: Initiative statute. Ca.gov. Retrieved from: http://primary98.sos.ca.gov/VoterGuide/Propositions/227text.htm.

BIBLIOGRAPHY

Callaghan, A.—quoted by Walters, L. S. (1996, May 23). US immigrants join rebellion to topple bilingual education. *Christian Science Monitor.* Retrieved from: https://www.csmonitor.com/1996/0523/052396.us.us.4.html.
Flake, J.—quoted by Zehr, M. A. (2001, February 21). Bush plan could alter bilingual education. *Education Week.* Retrieved from: https://www.edweek.org/teaching-learning/bush-plan-could-alter-bilingual-education/2001/02.
Title VII—Bilingual Education Programs, Public Law 90-247. (1968, January 2). U.S. Government. Retrieved from: https://www.govinfo.gov/content/pkg/STATUTE-81/pdf/STATUTE-81-Pg783.pdf.
Williams, C. P. (2021, December 8). A new federal equity agenda for dual language learners and English learners. Century Foundation. Retrieved from: https://tcf.org/content/report/new-federal-equity-agenda-dual-language-learners-english-learners/?agreed=1&agreed=1.

References for Expensive College Programs—Introduction

Korn, M., & Fuller, A. (2021, July 8). "Financially hobbled for life": The elite master's degrees that don't pay off. *Wall Street Journal.* Retrieved from: https://www.wsj.com/articles/financially-hobbled-for-life-the-elite-masters-degrees-that-dont-pay-off-11625752773.
Murphy, C. (2022, May 11). Student-loan forgiveness: "This focus on debt excuses the colleges for this dramatic increase in tuition." *Wall Street Journal.* Retrieved from: https://www.wsj.com/articles/notable-quotable-student-loan-forgiveness-college-debt-university-tuition-education-11652293571.
Restuccia, A., Lucey, C., & Andrews, N. (2022, June 18). Biden's long deliberations over some key policy decisions frustrate Democrats. *Wall Street Journal.* Retrieved from: https://www.wsj.com/articles/democrats-impatience-grows-as-they-await-biden-policy-decisions-11655557201.
Restuccia, A., & Rubin, G. T. (2022, June 6). Biden decision on student-loan forgiveness unlikely until later in summer, officials say. *Wall Street Journal.* Retrieved from: https://www.wsj.com/articles/biden-decision-on-student-loan-forgiveness-unlikely-until-later-in-summer-officials-say-11654542674.
Ringer, J., & Chakrabarti, M. (2022, May 2). The federal government's role in causing and fixing the student debt crisis. Wbur.org. Retrieved from: https://www.wbur.org/onpoint/2022/05/02/from-1994-to-today-heres-what-the-federal-government-has-done-that-led-to-1-7-trillion-in-student-loan-debt.
Smith, R., & Fuller, A., (2021, December 1). Some professional degrees leave students with high debt but without high salaries. *Wall Street Journal.* Retrieved from: https://www.wsj.com/articles/some-professional-degrees-leave-students-with-high-debt-but-without-high-salaries-11638354602.

BIBLIOGRAPHY

References for Expensive College Programs—Enthusiasts
Binkley, C. (2022, September 27). Biden's student debt plan would cost government $400B. *Florida Times-Union*. Retrieved from: https://jacksonville-fl-app.newsmemory.com/?publink=0491a945c_1348623.

Miller, B. (2020, January 13). Graduate school debt: Ideas for reducing the $37 billion in annual student loans that no one is talking about. Americanprogress.org. Retrieved from: https://www.americanprogress.org/article/graduate-school-debt.

Restuccia, A. (2022, May 23). As Biden zeroes in on student-loan forgiveness decision, voter anxiety grows. *Wall Street Journal*. Retrieved from: https://www.wsj.com/articles/as-biden-zeroes-in-on-student-loan-forgiveness-decision-voter-anxiety-grows-11653298200.

Restuccia, A., & Collins, E. (2022, April 26). Biden seriously considering student-loan forgiveness, officials say. *Wall Street Journal*. Retrieved from: https://www.wsj.com/articles/biden-seriously-considering-student-loan-forgiveness-officials-say-11651009143.

Sheffey, A. (2022, June 7). A top student-loan official says growing student debt loads for parents is "something we're watching very carefully"—but they may not be eligible for Biden's impending forgiveness plan. Businessinsider.com. Retrieved from: https://www.businessinsider.com/student-debt-parent-plus-loans-watched-carefully-kvaal-biden-forgiveness-2022-6.

References for Expensive College Programs—Skeptics
Douglas-Gabriel, D. (2020, February 13). Graduate school debt is driving up the cost of helping borrowers manage their student loans. *Washington Post*. Retrieved from: https://www.washingtonpost.com/education/2020/02/13/graduate-school-debt-is-driving-up-cost-helping-borrowers-manage-their-student-loans.

Fuller, A., Mitchell, J.,& Randazzo, S. (2021, August 3). Law school loses luster as debts mount and salaries stagnate. *Wall Street Journal*. Retrieved from: https://www.wsj.com/articles/law-school-student-debt-low-salaries-university-miami-11627991855.

Hurst, B. (2022, June 8). Student loan forgiveness makes my grandson a chump. *Wall Street Journal*. Retrieved from: https://www.wsj.com/articles/student-debt-forgiveness-makes-my-grandson-a-chump-summer-jobs-pay-loans-11654698177.

Minsky, A. S. (2022, June 8). 560,000 borrowers will get automatic student loan forgiveness, but others can still apply for relief. *Forbes*. Retrieved from: https://www.forbes.com/sites/adamminsky/2022/06/08/560000-borrowers-will-get-automatic-student-loan-forgiveness-but-others-can-still-apply-for-relief/?sh=1332ec035e83.

Todd, S. (2022, June 8). Is student loan forgiveness fair to everyone else? Qz.com. Retrieved from: https://qz.com/2175526/is-student-loan-debt-forgiveness-fair-to-everyone-else.

Wall Street Journal Editorial Board. (2022, September 27). Hooray, a student loan forgiveness plaintiff. *Wall Street Journal*. Retrieved from: https://www.wsj.com/articles/huzzah-a-student-loan-plaintiff-frank-garrison-lawsuit-biden-pacific-legal-foundation-11664311394.

BIBLIOGRAPHY

References for Expensive School Programs—Introduction

Asimov, N. (1998, May 5). English only alternate offered bill would let districts decide. *San Francisco Chronicle*. Retrieved from: https://www.sfgate.com/education/article/English-Only-Alternate-Offered-Bill-would-let-3006845.php.

Baker, C., & Wright, W. E. (2021). *Foundations of bilingual education and bilingualism.* Bristol, UK: Multilingual Matters.

Ballotpedia. (2016). California Proposition 58, non-English languages allowed in public education Retrieved from: https://ballotpedia.org/California_Proposition_58,_Non-English_Languages_Allowed_in_Public_Education_(2016).

California Legislative Analyst's Office. (2016, November 8). Proposition 58: English language education. Retrieved from: https://lao.ca.gov/BallotAnalysis/Proposition?number=58&year=2016.

California Proposition 227. (1998, June 2). English language in public schools: Initiative statute. Ca.gov. Retrieved from: http://primary98.sos.ca.gov/VoterGuide/Propositions/227text.htm.

Cardoza, K. (2021, February 24). Millions of kids learn English at school. Npr.org. Retrieved from: https://www.npr.org/2021/02/24/964420443/millions-of-kids-learn-english-at-school-teaching-them-remotely-hasnt-been-easy.

Frank, F. (1998, June 14). The California entrepreneur who beat bilingual teaching. *New York Times*. Retrieved from: https://www.nytimes.com/1998/06/14/us/the-california-entrepreneur-who-beat-bilingual-teaching.html.

Haver, J. J. (2013). *English for the children: Mandated by the people, skewed by politicians and special interests.* Lanham, MD: Rowman & Littlefield Education.

Ingram, N. (2018, October 30). In these bilingual classrooms, diversity is no longer lost in translation. *Christian Science Monitor*. Retrieved from: https://www.csmonitor.com/EqualEd/2018/1108/In-these-bilingual-classrooms-diversity-is-no-longer-lost-in-translation.

Kerr, E., & Wood, S., (2022, March 29). Is graduate school worth the cost? *U.S. New & World Report*. Retrieved from: https://www.usnews.com/education/best-graduate-schools/paying/articles/is-graduate-school-worth-the-cost.

Lopez, B. (2022, January 26). Gov. Greg Abbott taps into parent anger to fuel reelection campaign. *Texas Tribune*. Retrieved from: https://www.texastribune.org/2022/01/26/greg-abbott-parental-bill-of-rights.

Powell, E. (2016, October 26). Do California parents want bilingual education? *Christian Science Monitor*. Retrieved from: https://www.csmonitor.com/USA/Education/2016/1026/Do-California-parents-want-bilingual-education.

Renee, A. (2016, November 9). Prop 58: Higher demand for bilingual teachers not helping teacher shortage. Abc10.com. Retrieved from: https://www.abc10.com/article/news/local/california/prop-58-higher-demand-for-bilingual-teachers-not-helping-teacher-shortage/103-350584412.

Sanchez, C. (2016, November 25). Bilingual education returns to California: Now what? Npr.org. Retrieved from: https://www.npr.org/sections/ed/2016/11/25/502904113/bilingual-education-returns-to-california-now-what.

References for Expensive School Programs—Enthusiasts
Children at risk. (2022). PK-12 Education. Childrenatrisk.org. Retrieved from: https://childrenatrisk.org/education.

Dangers of "English-only" policies (for ESL students) in school. (2019, August 1). Ethicalesol.org. Retrieved from: https://www.ethicalesol.org/blog/hhryxasqrobl9b8gzcza24aj6x5w5q.

Merl, J. (1998, May 10). L.A. Latinos join forces to save bilingual classes. *Los Angeles Times*. Retrieved from: https://www.latimes.com/archives/la-xpm-1998-may-10-me-48283-story.html.

School officials say Prop. 227 could cost area $100 million. (1998, May 15). *Los Angeles Times*. Retrieved from: https://www.latimes.com/archives/la-xpm-1998-may-15-me-50053-story.html.

Stavley, Z. (2022, January 24). How Congress can help students learning English. Edsource.org. Retrieved from: https://edsource.org/2022/how-congress-can-help-students-learning-english/666330.

Williams, C. P. (2020, March 31). The case for expanding federal funding for English learners. Tcf.org. Retrieved from: https://tcf.org/content/commentary/case-expanding-federal-funding-english-learners/?session=1.

References for Expensive School Programs—Skeptics
Asian-American elected officials and community leaders endorse Proposition 227. (1998, April 9). Onenation.org. Retrieved from: https://www.onenation.org/pr040998.html.

Pedalino Porter, R. (1998, May). The case against bilingual education. *The Atlantic*. Retrieved from: https://www.theatlantic.com/magazine/archive/1998/05/the-case-against-bilingual-education/305426.

Pyle, A. (1996, February 13). Latino parents to boycott school bilingual plan. *Los Angeles Times*. Retrieved from: https://www.latimes.com/archives/la-xpm-1996-02-13-me-35409-story.html.

Pyle, A. (1996, February 14). 80 students stay out of school in Latino boycott. *Los Angeles Times*. Retrieved from: https://www.latimes.com/archives/la-xpm-1996-02-13-me-35409-story.html.

Tini, T. (1998, April 10). Asian American leaders endorse Prop. 227. *Los Angeles Times*. Retrieved from: http://articles.latimes.com/1998/apr/10/local/me-37976.

REFERENCES FOR CHAPTER 9
References for Chapter 9 Epigraphs
American Civil Liberties Union Florida. (2022). School to prison pipeline: Local resources. Retrieved from: https://www.aclufl.org/en/school-prison-pipeline-local-resources.

American Psychological Association Zero Tolerance Task Force. (2008, December). Are zero tolerance policies effective in the schools: An evidentiary review and recommendations. American Psychological Association. Retrieved from:

Bibliography

chrome-extension://efaidnbmnnnibpcajpcglclefindmkaj/https://www.apa.org/pubs/reports/zero-tolerance.pdf.

Emmanuel, B. (2022). Effects of zero tolerance policies in schools. Adayinourshoes.com. Retrieved from: https://adayinourshoes.com/zero-tolerance-policy-special-education.

Gjelten, E. A. (2019, February 5). What are zero tolerance policies in schools? Lawyers.com. Retrieved from: https://www.lawyers.com/legal-info/research/education-law/whats-a-zero-tolerance-policy.html.

State of Florida. (2022). Florida Statutes, 2022 Title XLVIII: Early Learning-20 Education Code. Retrieved from: http://www.leg.state.fl.us/statutes/index.cfm?App_mode=Display_Statute&Search_String=&URL=1000-1099/1006/Sections/1006.13.html.

References for Supermarket Policies—Introduction

AImazing.co. (2021 January 13). How grocery stores and supermarkets are making use of data analytics. Retrieved from: https://www.aimazing.co/post/how-grocery-stores-and-supermarkets-are-making-use-of-data-analytics#gref.

Castelli, P. (2022). Grocery data analytics and planning: Ensuring availability and maximizing performance. Blog.board.com. Retrieved from: https://blog.board.com/bi-analytics-reporting/grocery-data-analytics-planning/1544.

Czerny, A. I. (2008). *Airport slots: International experiences and options for reform*. Aldershot, UK: Ashgate.

Czerny, A. I. (2016). *Airport slots: International experiences and options for reform*. London: Routledge,

McMahon, M. (2022, August 7). What is a slotting fee? Aboutmechanics.com. Retrieved from: https://www.aboutmechanics.com/what-is-a-slotting-fee.htm.

PPCexpo. (2022). Examples of marketing analytics: Real-life challenges while doing analysis in PPC. Retrieved from: https://ppcexpo.com/blog/examples-of-marketing-analytics.

Shimp, T. A., & Andrews, J. C. (2013). *Advertising, promotion, and other aspects of integrated marketing communications*. Mason, OH: Cengage Learning.

References for Supermarket Policies—Enthusiasts

Aalberts, R. J., & Jennings, M. M. (1999, July). The ethics of slotting: Is this bribery, facilitation marketing or just plain competition? *Journal of Business Ethics*. Retrieved from: https://www.jstor.org/stable/25074132.

Bedrock Analytics. (2019, August 14). What goes into a slotting fee? Retrieved from: https://www.bedrockanalytics.com/blog/what-goes-into-a-slotting-fee.

Tabor, M. B. (1996, January 15). Bookstore chains, display space is for sale. *New York Times*. Retrieved from: https://www.nytimes.com/1996/01/15/us/in-bookstore-chains-display-space-is-for-sale.html.

Traxretail.com. (2019, June). Quick guide to shelf space costs. Retrieved from: https://traxretail.com/blog/quick-guide-shelf-space-costs.

Bibliography

References for Supermarket Policies—Skeptics
Bloom, P. N., Gundlach, G. T., & Cannon, J. P. (2000, April). Slotting allowances and fees: Schools of thought and the views of practicing managers. *Journal of Marketing.* Retrieved from: https://journals.sagepub.com/doi/10.1509/jmkg.64.2.92.18002.

Edwards, P. (2016, November 22). The hidden war over grocery shelf space: It determines what you buy in the grocery—long before you get a look at the shelf. Vox.com. Retrieved from: https://www.vox.com/2016/11/22/13707022/grocery-store-slotting-fees-slotting-allowances.

Gilbert, D. (2018, December 6). Slotting fees: What suppliers need to know. Dotactiv.com. Retrieved from: https://www.dotactiv.com/blog/slotting-fees.

References for Disability Policies—Introduction
Clint, F. (2022). Zero tolerance policies & special education. Study.com. Retrieved from: https://study.com/academy/lesson/zero-tolerance-policies-special-education.html#:~:text=A%20zero%20tolerance%20policy%20is,manifestation%20of%20a%20student's%20disability.

Kafka, J. (2016). *History of zero tolerance in American public schooling.* New York: Palgrave Macmillan.

Mitchell, K. (2018). We can't tolerate that behavior in this school: The consequences of excluding children with behavioral health conditions and the limits of the law. *N.Y.U. Review of Law & Social Change.* Retrieved from: https://socialchangenyu.com/review/we-cant-tolerate-that-behavior-in-this-school-the-consequences-of-excluding-children-with-behavioral-health-conditions-and-the-limits-of-the-law.

Sippl, A. (2022, June). The ABA Controversy. Appliedbehavioranalysisprograms.com. Retrieved from: https://www.appliedbehavioranalysisprograms.com/faq/controversy-surrounding-aba.

Terrazas, E. (2009). *When my child is disciplined at school: A guide for families.* Senate.texas.gov. Retrieved from: https://senate.texas.gov/cmtes/81/c530/SB33-EricaTerrazas-1.pdf.

Virginia Division of Special Education and Student Services. (2010). Discipline of children with disabilities: Technical assistance resources document. Retrieved from: https://www.doe.virginia.gov/support/student_conduct/discipline_children_disabilities.pdf.

References for Disability Policies—Enthusiasts
Florida compilation of school discipline laws and regulations. (2021, March 31). Safesupportivelearning.ed.gov. Retrieved from: https://safesupportivelearning.ed.gov/sites/default/files/discipline-compendium/Florida%20School%20Discipline%20Laws%20and%20Regulations.pdf.

Florida Department of Juvenile Justice. (2009, April 29). Zero tolerance bill passes full senate. Florida Department of Juvenile Justice. Retrieved from: https://www.djj.state.fl.us/news/press-releases/2009/zero-tolerance-bill-passes-full-senate.

Florida House of Representatives. (2011). School safety and student discipline. Retrieved from: https://www.myfloridahouse.gov/FileStores/Web/HouseContent/Approved/Web%20Site/education_fact_sheets/2011/documents/2010-11%20School%20Safety%20and%20Student%20Discipline.3.pdf.

References for Disability Policies—Skeptics

Albite, K. (2014, March 10). Zero tolerance policies in Florida schools: Shifting from incapacitation to rehabilitation. *University of Miami Law Review.* Retrieved from: https://lawreview.law.miami.edu/tolerance-policies-florida-schools-shifting-incapacitation-rehabilitation.

Cerrone, K. M. (1999). The Gun-Free Schools Act of 1994: Zero tolerance takes aim at procedural due process. *Pace Law Review.* Retrieved from: http://digitalcommons.pace.edu/cgi/viewcontent.cgi?article=1265&context=plr.

Federal Trade Commission. (2003, November 14). FTC Releases grocery industry slotting allowance report. Retrieved from: https://www.ftc.gov/news-events/news/press-releases/2003/11/ftc-releases-grocery-industry-slotting-allowance-report.

Fredla.org. (2016, January). Students with disabilities & the juvenile justice system: What parents need to know. Retrieved from: https://fredla.org/wp-content/uploads/2016/01/JJ-8.pdf.

Klein, B., & Wright, J. D. (2006, November 8). The economics of slotting contracts. U.S. Department of Justice. Retrieved from: https://www.justice.gov/atr/economics-slotting-contracts.

Leifertlaw.com. (2010). Florida Law Enforcement Blog. Retrieved from: https://www.leifertlaw.com/blog/south-florida-lawyers-discuss-schools-zero-tolerance-laws.

Maxime, F. (2018, January 1). Zero-tolerance policies and the school to prison pipeline. Sharedjustice.org. Retrieved from: https://www.sharedjustice.org/most-recent/2017/12/21/zero-tolerance-policies-and-the-school-to-prison-pipeline.

MST Services. (2018, September 18). How can we stop the school-to-prison pipeline? (2018, September 18). Mstservices.com. https://info.mstservices.com/blog/can-we-stop-the-school-to-prison-pipeline.

Ruth, Z., & Julia, D. B. (2002, December 31). The children left behind: How zero tolerance impacts our most vulnerable youth. *Michigan Journal of Race and Law.* Retrieved from: https://repository.law.umich.edu/cgi/viewcontent.cgi?article=1170&context=mjrl.

Sherman, A. (2013, July 30). "Over 12,000 school kids were arrested in Florida: It makes Florida the nation's leader in that area," says Dream Defenders. Politifact.com. Retrieved from: https://www.politifact.com/factchecks/2013/jul/30/dream-defenders/over-12000-school-kids-were-arrested-florida-it-ma.

Tebo, M. G. (2000, April). Zero tolerance, zero sense. U.S. Office of Justice Programs. Retrieved from: https://www.ojp.gov/ncjrs/virtual-library/abstracts/zero-tolerance-zero-sense.

Whitehead, J. W. (1999, July 19). Student sentenced to one-year expulsion for possession of nail clippers. Rutherford.org. Retrieved from: https://www.rutherford.org/

publications_resources/john_whiteheads_commentary/student_sentenced_to_one_year_expulsion_for_possession_of_nail_clippers.

Winter, C. (2022). Amid evidence zero tolerance doesn't work, schools reverse themselves. Apmreports.org. Retrieved from: https://www.apmreports.org/episode/2016/08/25/reforming-school-discipline.

REFERENCES FOR CHAPTER 10
References for Beginning-of-Chapter-10 Quotes

Chicago Teachers Union.—quoted by *Wall Street Journal* Editorial Board. (2021, December 30). The Chicago Teachers Union's priorities. *Wall Street Journal*. Retrieved from: https://www.wsj.com/articles/the-chicago-teachers-unions-priorities-students-public-schools-strike-pedro-martinez-11640903743?mod=hp_opin_pos_3#cxrecs_s.

Chicago Teachers Union.—from a photo by Dabrowski, T., & Klingner, J. (2022, January 14). Why the Chicago Teachers Union always gets what it wants. *Wall Street Journal*. Retrieved from: https://www.wsj.com/articles/chicago-teachers-union-gets-what-it-wants-strike-students-covid-teaching-education-omicron-collective-bargianing-11642199401?mod=hp_opin_pos_3#cxrecs_s.

Dunn, N.—quoted by Mogos, A. (2022, January 8). Parents frustrated as teachers refuse to work in-person, district cancels classes. Wttw.com. Retrieved from: https://news.wttw.com/2022/01/08/parents-frustrated-teachers-refuse-work-person-district-cancels-classes.

Lightfoot, L.—quoted by Barrett, J., & Council, S. (2022, January 11). Chicago's parents prove to be key in getting schools back in session. *Wall Street Journal*. Retrieved from: https://www.wsj.com/articles/chicagos-parents-prove-to-be-key-in-getting-schools-back-in-session-11641938024.

Stryker, B.—quoted by Riccardi, N., & Binkley, C. (2022, January 14). Democrats at odds over school closures. *Florida Times-Union*. Retrieved from: https://jacksonville-fl-app.newsmemory.com/?publink=22147746c_13482f6.

References for Gaslighting at College—Introduction

Emamzadeh, A. (2022, January 30). Surprising new findings on power and gaslighting. *Psychology Today*. Retrieved from: https://www.psychologytoday.com/us/blog/finding-new-home/202201/surprising-new-findings-power-and-gaslighting.

Halliday, A. (2022, January 14). The origins of the word "gaslighting": Scenes from the 1944 film *Gaslight*. Openculture.com. Retrieved from: https://www.openculture.com/2022/01/the-origins-of-the-word-gaslighting-scenes-from-the-1944-film.html.

Huizen, J. (2020, July 14). What is gaslighting? Medicalnewstoday.com. Retrieved from: https://www.medicalnewstoday.com/articles/gaslighting.

Maureen, M. (1995, November 26). Liberties: The gaslight strategy. *New York Times*. Retrieved from: https://www.nytimes.com/1995/11/26/opinion/l-liberties-the-gaslight-strategy-066192.html.

Bibliography

Pettit, E. (2021, December 16). When professors offend students: Classroom norms are changing. *Chronicle of Higher Education*. Retrieved from: https://www.chronicle.com/article/when-professors-offend-students.

Schlosser, E. (2015, June 3). I'm a liberal professor, and my liberal students terrify me. Vox.com. Retrieved from: https://www.vox.com/2015/6/3/8706323/college-professor-afraid.

References for Gaslighting at College—Enthusiasts

California Legislature. (2014). AB-2053—Employment discrimination or harassment: Education and training: Abusive conduct. Retrieved from: https://leginfo.legislature.ca.gov/faces/billTextClient.xhtml?bill_id=201320140AB2053.

Mayshark, L. (2018). Gaslighting and academic bullying in college can lead to PTSD (2018). Lorenmayshark.com. Retrieved from: https://lorenmayshark.com/gaslighting-and-academic-bullying-can-lead-to-ptsd.

Patterson, M. (2019, June 4). Overcoming gaslighting in a higher education setting. Ombuds.medium.com. Retrieved from: https://ombuds.medium.com/overcoming-gaslighting-in-higher-education-bff81a45def7.

Peña, E. S. (2018, February 24). Surviving mean professors and negative criticism. Mystudentvoices.com. Retrieved from: https://mystudentvoices.com/surviving-mean-professors-and-negative-criticism-a93354f0b4dd.

Saint Mary's College of California. (2022). Gaslighting—What does it mean? Retrieved from: https://www.stmarys-ca.edu/sexual-assault-and-violence-prevention/gaslighting-what-does-it-mean.

University of California. (2016, July 16). Workplace bullying policy. Retrieved from: https://m.box.com/shared_item/https%3A%2F%2Fucla.box.com%2Fv%2Fbully-policy.

University of California Los Angeles. (2016, September 2). Guidance on abusive behavior in the workplace. Retrieved from: https://chr.ucla.edu/policies-and-labor-contracts/uidance-on-abusive-behavior-in-the-workplace.

References for Gaslighting at College—Skeptics

Artze-Vega, I. (2014, December 8). Cruel student comments: Seven ways to soothe the sting. Facultyfocus.com. Retrieved from: https://www.facultyfocus.com/articles/faculty-development/cruel-student-comments-seven-ways-soothe-sting.

Lawrence, J. W. (2018, May-June). Student evaluations of teaching are not valid. Aaup.org. Retrieved from: https://www.aaup.org/article/student-evaluations-teaching-are-not-valid#.YzspL-zMI6E.

Lynch, M. (2021, June 13). The gaslighting of teachers, professors, and education administrators: The elephant in the room. Theedadvocate.org. Retrieved from: https://www.theedadvocate.org/the-gaslighting-of-teachers-professors-and-education-administrators-the-elephant-in-the-room.

Panchapakesan, A. (2021, November 6). UCLA students discuss how institutions, individuals gaslight racial groups. Dailybruin.com. Retrieved from: https://dailybruin

.com/2021/11/06/the-quad-ucla-students-discuss-how-institutions-individuals-gaslight-racial-groups.

Saad, G. (2011, November 17). Students criticizing professors online: A right or a violation? *Psychology Today*. Retrieved from: https://www.psychologytoday.com/us/blog/homo-consumericus/201111/students-criticizing-professors-online-right-or-violation.

Schmidt, P. (2017, January 13). When students' prejudices taint reviews of instructors. *Chronicle of Higher Education*. Retrieved from: https://www.chronicle.com/article/when-students-prejudices-taint-reviews-of-instructors.

References for Gaslighting in Public Schools—Introduction

Chicago Public Schools. (2022). Pedro Martinez, Chief Executive Officer. Retrieved from: https://www.cps.edu/about/leadership/chief-executive-officer/#:~:text=Pedro%20Martinez%2C%20Chief%20Executive%20Officer%20%7C%20Chicago%20Public%20Schools.

Dailey, R. (2021, December 17). Florida-federal feud ends over school mask mandates. *Florida Times-Union*. Retrieved from: https://jacksonville-fl-app.newsmemory.com/?publink=5a336b572_1346035.

Fung, K. (2021, December 21). "The Great Exodus": Superintendents resigned in droves as culture wars hit schools. *Newsweek*. Retrieved from: https://www.newsweek.com/great-exodus-superintendents-resigned-droves-culture-wars-hit-schools-2021-1662382.

Giordano, G. (2003). *Twentieth-century textbook wars: A history of advocacy and opposition*. New York: P. Lang.

Giordano, G. (2019). *Parents and textbooks: Answers that reveal essential steps for improvement*. Lanham, MD: Rowman & Littlefield.

Morris, B., & Calfas, J. (2022, January 5). Omicron school disruptions stress already-frayed parents—Again. *Wall Street Journal*. Retrieved from: https://www.wsj.com/articles/omicron-school-disruptions-stress-already-frayed-parentsagain-11641378604.

Nazaryan, A. (2022, January 5). "We want schools to be open," White House says as Chicago cancels classes. News.yahoo.com. Retrieved from: https://news.yahoo.com/we-want-schools-to-be-open-white-house-says-as-chicago-cancels-classes-201418110.html.

Simon, C. (2021, December 13). State leaders have hamstrung schools on taking on COVID-19. *Florida Times-Union*. Retrieved from: https://jacksonville-fl-app.newsmemory.com/?publink=187021f58_1346031.

Williams, C. (2022, January 8). Return to remote learning leaves families in despair. *Florida Times-Union*. Retrieved from: https:jacksonville-fl-app.newsmemory.com/?publink=037bfb971_13482f0.

References for Gaslighting in Public Schools—Enthusiasts

Barrett, J., & Council, S. (2022, January 11). Chicago's parents prove to be key in getting schools back in session. *Wall Street Journal*. Retrieved from: https://www

.wsj.com/articles/chicagos-parents-prove-to-be-key-in-getting-schools-back-in-session-11641938024.

References for Gaslighting in Public Schools—Skeptics

Barrett, J. (2021, May 3). Chicago Public Schools CEO Janice Jackson to step down. *Wall Street Journal.* Retrieved from: https://www.wsj.com/articles/chicago-public-schools-ceo-janice-jackson-to-step-down-11620072126.

Campuzano, E. (2021, November 30). "We just can't support that": Portland Public Schools leaders respond to union's virtual instruction proposal. *Oregonian.* Retrieved from https://www.oregonlive.com/education/2021/12/we-just-cant-support-that-portland-public-schools-leaders-respond-to-unions-virtual-instruction-proposal.html.

Dorman, S. (2021, May 3). Chicago Public Schools CEO becomes latest of several top officials to resign. *Fox News.* Retrieved from: https://www.foxnews.com/us/chicago-public-schools-ceo-resigns.

Freeman, J. (2022, January 5). Are Chicago students suffering with or from teachers unions? *Wall Street Journal.* Retrieved from: https://www.wsj.com/articles/are-chicago-students-suffering-with-or-from-teachers-unions-11641414392?mod=hp_opin_pos_3#cxrecs_s.

Masterson, M. (2022, January 8). Chicago parents suing CTU in push to get kids back in their classrooms. News.wttw.com. Retrieved from: https://news.wttw.com/2022/01/08/chicago-parents-suing-ctu-push-get-kids-back-their-classrooms.

Masterson, M. (2022, January 10). Students set to return to classroom as Chicago teachers suspend labor action. News.wttw.com. Retrieved from: https://news.wttw.com/2022/01/10/students-set-return-classroom-chicago-teachers-suspend-labor-action.

Meckler, L. (2022, January 14). National School Boards Association stumbles into politics and is blasted apart. *Washington Post.* Retrieved from: https://www.washingtonpost.com/education/2022/01/13/school-board-association-domestic-terrorism.

Riccardi, N., & Binkley, C. (2022, January 14). Democrats at odds over school closures. *Florida Times-Union.* Retrieved from: https://jacksonville-fl-app.newsmemory.com/?publink=22147746c_13482f6.

Wall Street Journal Editorial Board (2021, December 30). The Chicago Teachers Union's priorities. *Wall Street Journal.* Retrieved from: https://www.wsj.com/articles/the-chicago-teachers-unions-priorities-students-public-schools-strike-pedro-martinez-11640903743?mod=hp_opin_pos_3#cxrecs_s.

Wall Street Journal Editorial Board. (2022, January 5). The scandal of Chicago's teachers union. *Wall Street Journal.* Retrieved from: https://www.wsj.com/articles/the-scandal-of-chicagos-teachers-union-doug-ducey-arizona-schools-students-covid-11641422073?mod=hp_opin_pos_4#cxrecs_s.

REFERENCES FOR CHAPTER 11
References for Chapter 11 Epigraphs
Anderson, N. (2021, April 20). Siblings: A military brat's best friends. Militaryonesource.mil. Retrieved from: https://blog-brigade.militaryonesource.mil/2021/04/20/siblings-a-military-brats-best-friends.

Arndt, S. (2022). Children of deployed military parents more at risk for alcohol, drug use. University of Iowa Healthcare. Retrieved from: https://medicine.uiowa.edu/psychiatry/content/children-deployed-military-parents-more-risk-alcohol-drug-use.

Butler Center for Research. (2018, May). Substance use disorder among military populations. *Journal of the American Medical Association Pediatrics*. Retrieved from: https://www.hazeldenbettyford.org/education/bcr/addiction-research/substance-abuse-military-ru-518.

Sogomonyan, F., & Cooper, J. L. (2010, May). Trauma faced by children of military families: what every policymaker should know. National Center for Children in Poverty. Retrieved from: https://www.nccp.org/publication/trauma-faced-by-children-of-military-families/#:~:text=Children%20in%20military%20families%20experience,many%20children%20in%20military%20families.

Unidentified Child.—quoted by Kavitha Cardoza, K. (2019, January 22). Schools strive to support the unique needs of military children. Pbs.org. Retrieved from: https://www.pbs.org/newshour/show/schools-strive-to-support-the-unique-needs-of-military-children.

U.S. Institute of Medicine (2014). Preventing psychological disorders in service members and their families: An assessment of programs. In *Returning home from Iraq and Afghanistan: Assessment of readjustment needs of veterans, service members, and their families*. Washington, DC: National Academies Press.

References for Urban Crime Syndrome.—Introduction
Atkinson, R., & Millington, G. (2019). *Urban criminology: The city, disorder harm and social control*. New York: Routledge/Taylor & Francis.

Barnett, O. W., & LaViolette, A. D. (1996). Battered woman syndrome is a legitimate defense. U.S. Department of Justice. Retrieved from: https://www.ojp.gov/ncjrs/virtual-library/abstracts/battered-woman-syndrome-legitimate-defense-violence-opposing.

Wikström, P. H. (2013). *Breaking rules: The social and situational dynamics of young people's urban crime*. Oxford, UK: Oxford University Press.

Zdanowicz, C. (2019, November 11). His dad has been deployed 10 times. CNN. Retrieved from: https://www.cnn.com/2019/11/10/us/military-family-life-dad-deployed-trnd/index.html.

References for Urban Crime Syndrome—Enthusiasts
Allen, R. C. (1996, July). Socioeconomic conditions and property crime: a comprehensive review and test of the professional literature. *American Journal of Economics and*

Sociology. Retrieved from: https://onlinelibrary.wiley.com/doi/abs/10.1111/j.1536-7150.1996.tb02311.

Caliendo, S. M. (2022). *Inequality in America: Race, poverty, and fulfilling democracy's promise.* New York/London: Routledge/Taylor & Francis.

Ceccato, V. (2012). *The urban fabric of crime and fear.* Netherlands: Springer.

References for Urban Crime Syndrome—Skeptics

Giordano, G. (2022). *Parents and school violence: Essential steps to improve schools.* Lanham, MD: Rowman & Littlefield.

Howsen, R. M., & Jarrell, S. B. (1987, October). Some determinants of property crime: Economic factors influence criminal behavior but cannot completely explain the Syndrome. *American Journal of Economics and Sociology.* Retrieved from: https://onlinelibrary.wiley.com/doi/abs/10.1111/j.1536-7150.1987.tb01992.

References for Military Family Syndrome—Introduction

Anderson, N. (2021, April 20). Siblings: A military brat's best friends. Militaryonesource.mil. Retrieved from: https://blog-brigade.militaryonesource.mil/2021/04/20/siblings-a-military-brats-best-friends.

Blaisure, K., Saathoff-Wells, T., Pereira, A., Wadsworth, S. M. D., & Dombro, A. L. (2016). *Serving military families: Theories, research, and application.* New York: Routledge.

Bogen, J. (2019, March 28). The dismal career opportunities for military spouses. *The Atlantic.* Retrieved from: https://www.theatlantic.com/family/archive/2019/03/majority-military-spouses-are-underemployed/585586.

Butler Center for Research. (2018, May). Substance use disorder among military populations. *Journal of the American Medical Association Pediatrics.* Retrieved from: https://www.hazeldenbettyford.org/education/bcr/addiction-research/substance-abuse-military-ru-518.

Chandra, A., Lara-Cinisomo, S., Jaycox, L. H., Tanielian, T., Burns, R. M., Ruder, T., & Han, B. (2010). Children on the homefront: The experience of children from military families. *Pediatrics,* 125(1), 16–25.

De Pedro, K., Esqueda, M., Cederbaum, J., & Astor, R. A. (2014). District, school, and community stakeholder perspectives on the experiences of military-connected students. *Teachers College Record,* 116(5):1–32.

Farley, J. I. (2016). *Military 101: Basic training for new military families.* Lanham, MD: Rowman & Littlefield.

Gewirtz, A. H., & Youssef, A. M. (Eds.). (2016). *Parenting and children's resilience in military families.* New York: Springer.

Lagrone, D. M. (1978, September). The military family syndrome. *American Journal of Psychiatry.* Retrieved from: https://pubmed.ncbi.nlm.nih.gov/696922.

References for Military Family Syndrome—Enthusiasts

Blaisure, K. (2016). *Serving military families: Theories research and application* (2nd ed.). New York: Routledge.

Collins, E. M. (2015, May 6). Experts explain mental state of military children. U.S. Army. Retrieved from: https://www.army.mil/article/147786/experts_explain_mental_state_of_military_children.

Green, C. (2015, August 18). Children in military families more likely to have problems. Healthline.com. Retrieved from: https://www.healthline.com/health-news/children-in-military-families-more-likely-to-have-problems-081715.

Gruzewski, K. (2020). *Therapy games for teens: 150 activities to improve self-esteem communication and coping skills.* Emeryville, CA: Rockridge.

Hall, L. K. (2008). *Counseling military families: What mental health professionals need to know.* New York: Routledge.

Lawhorne, C., Philpott, D., & Scott, J. (2014). *Raising children in the military.* Lanham, MD: Rowman & Littlefield.

Mates-Youngman K. (2021). *The family therapy workbook: 96 guided interventions to help families connect cope and heal.* Eau Claire, WI: PESI.

Murphey, D. (2013, July 22). 5 risks facing young children in military families. *Child Trends.* Retrieved from: https://www.childtrends.org/publications/5-risks-facing-young-children-in-our-military-families.

Snyder, D. K. & Monson C. M. (2012). *Couple-based interventions for military and veteran families: A practitioner's guide.* New York: Guilford.

Sogomonyan, F., & Cooper, J. L. (2010, May). Trauma faced by children of military families: What every policymaker should know. National Center for Children in Poverty. Retrieved from: https://www.nccp.org/publication/trauma-faced-by-children-of-military-families/#:~:text=Children%20in%20military%20families%20experience,many%20children%20in%20military%20families.

Stebnicki, M. A. (2020). *Clinical military counseling: Guidelines for practice.* Alexandria, VA: American Counseling Association.

U.S. Department of Defense. (2022). Exceptional Family Member. Militaryonesource.mil. Retrieved from: https://www.militaryonesource.mil/family-relationships/special-needs/exceptional-family-member.

U.S. Department of Defense. (2022, July 20). See what's new with the Exceptional Family Member Program. Militaryonesource.mil. Retrieved from: https://www.militaryonesource.mil/family-relationships/special-needs/exceptional-family-member/new-efmp-tools-and-resources.

References for Military Family Syndrome—Skeptics

Fernandez, B. (1988, August). Does the military family syndrome exist? *Military Medicine.* Retrieved from: https://academic.oup.com/milmed/article-abstract/153/8/418/4846937.

REFERENCES FOR CHAPTER 12
References for Chapter 12 Epigraphs
Abbott, G.—quoted by McGee, K. (2022, May 5). Gov. Greg Abbott says federal government should cover cost of educating undocumented students in Texas public schools. *Texas Tribune*. Retrieved from: https://www.texastribune.org/2022/05/05/greg-abbott-plyler-doe-education/amp.

Hernandez, S. (2020, December 7). Border Patrol sees increase in abandoned infants, toddlers at the border. Borderreport.com. Retrieved from: https://www.borderreport.com/hot-topics/immigration/exclusive-border-patrol-sees-increase-in-abandoned-infants-toddlers-at-the-border.

Gramlich, J., & Scheller, A. (2021, November 9). What's happening at the U.S.—Mexico border in 7 charts. Pewresearch.org. Retrieved from: https://www.pewresearch.org/fact-tank/2021/11/09/whats-happening-at-the-u-s-mexico-border-in-7-charts.

Moreno, M.—quoted by Hennessy-Fiske, M. (2014, September 15). Texas schools struggle to serve huge number of immigrants. Governing.com. Retrieved from: https://www.governing.com/news/headlines/texas-schools-struggle-to-serve-influx-of-immigrants.html.

Paxton, K.—quoted by Glynn, M. (2022, April 26). Texas House lawmakers weigh impact of migrant influx on public schools. Kxan.com. Retrieved from: https://www.kxan.com/news/texas-politics/texas-house-lawmakers-weigh-impact-of-migrant-influx-on-public-schools.

Saenz, T.—quoted by McGee, K. (2022, May 5). Gov. Greg Abbott says federal government should cover cost of educating undocumented students in Texas public schools. *Texas Tribune*. Retrieved from: https://www.texastribune.org/2022/05/05/greg-abbott-plyler-doe-education/amp.

References for Educating Teens in NYC—Introduction
Algar, S., Brown, L., & Campanile, C. (2021, October 8). NYC to phase out gifted and talented program. *New York Post*. Retrieved from: https://nypost.com/2021/10/08/nyc-to-phase-out-gifted-and-talented-program.

Elsen-Rooney, M. (2017, November 8). Mysterious bonus makes rich NYC schools richer, critics say. Wnyc.org. Retrieved from: https://www.wnyc.org/story/mysterious-bonus-makes-rich-nyc-schools-richer-critics-say.

Giordano, G. (2005). *How testing came to dominate American schools: The history of educational assessment*. New York: P. Lang.

Giordano, G. (2009). *Solving education's problems effectively: A guide to using the case method*. Lanham, MD: Rowman & Littlefield.

Giordano, G. (2011). *Capping cost: Putting a price tag on school reform*. Lanham, MD: Roman & Littlefield.

Giordano, G. (2011). *Lopsided schools: Case method briefings*. Lanham, MD: Rowman & Littlefield.

Giordano, G. (2016). *Common sense questions about tests: The answers can reveal essential steps for improvement*. Lanham, MD: Rowman & Littlefield.

BIBLIOGRAPHY

Linge, M. K. (2021, December 9). High school guide: The specialized Elite 8. *New York Post*. Retrieved from: https://nypost.com/2021/12/09/high-school-guide-the-specialized-elite-8.

New York City Department of Education. (2022). Specialized High School Admissions Test. Retrieved from: https://www.schools.nyc.gov/learning/testing/specialized-high-school-admissions-test.

New York State Assembly. (2018, April 20). Memorandum In Support of Legislation: Submitted in accordance with Assembly Rule III, Sec 1(f). Retrieved from: https://nyassembly.gov/leg/?default_fld=&leg_video=&bn=A10427&term=2017&Memo=Y&Text=Y.

Testingmom.com. (2022). New York City Specialized High Schools: The Elite 8 high schools that require the SHSAT. Retrieved from: https://www.testingmom.com/tests/shsat/new-york-city-specialized-high-schools.

References for Educating Teens in NYC—Enthusiasts

A-List Education. (2021, October 13). 5 SHSAT Controversies. Retrieved from: https://alisteducation.com/blog/5-shsat-controversies.

Linge, M. K. (2022, April 16). Why today's youth are no longer starstruck by NYC "Fame School." *New York Post*. Retrieved from: https://nypost.com/2022/04/16/laguardia-fame-school-doesnt-impress-todays-youth.

Sunset the SHSAT. (2022). Retrieved from: https://shsatsunset.org.

References for Educating Teens in NYC—Skeptics

Knudson, A. (2019, June 17). Report: New York senator calls for more specialized high schools. Silive.com. Retrieved from: https://www.silive.com/news/2019/06/report-new-york-senator-calls-for-more-specialized-high-schools.html.

Knudson, A. (2022, April 11). NYC Mayor Eric Adams suggests creating new specialized high schools in each borough, report says. Silive.com. Retrieved from: https://www.silive.com/education/2022/04/nyc-mayor-eric-adams-suggests-creating-new-specialized-high-schools-in-each-borough-report-says.html.

Li, M. (2022, April 4). I wanted to know what my high school peers thought about the SHSAT, so I asked them. Chalkbeat.org. Retrieved from: https://ny.chalkbeat.org/2022/4/4/23003866/shsat-asian-students-specialized-high-school-admissions.

NY1.com. (2019, September 25). "Our plan didn't work": De Blasio indicates openness to keeping the SHSAT. Retrieved from: https://www.ny1.com/nyc/all-boroughs/politics/2019/09/26/shsat-bill-de-blasio-says-plan-to-scrap-specialized-high-school-exam-did-not-work.

Riley, J. L. (2022, March 1). Asian-Americans fight back against school discrimination. *Wall Street Journal*. Retrieved from: https://www.wsj.com/articles/asian-american-fight-school-discrimination-affirmative-action-racial-justice-admissions-standards-testing-charter-schools-achievement-gap-harvard-supreme-court-11646172518.

BIBLIOGRAPHY

References for Educating Migrants in Texas—Introduction

Chen, G. (2022, May 7). Public schools struggle to accommodate unaccompanied migrant children Publicschoolreview.com. Retrieved from: https://www.publicschoolreview.com/blog/public-schools-struggle-to-accommodate-unaccompanied-migrant-children.

Constitutional Rights Foundation. (2022). History lesson 10: *Plyler v. Doe*: Can states deny public benefits to illegal immigrants? Retrieved from: http://crfimmigrationed.org/lessons-for-teachers/149-hl10.

Gramlich, J. (2021, August 13). Migrant encounters at U.S.—Mexico border are at a 21-year high. Pewresearch.org. Retrieved from: https://www.pewresearch.org/fact-tank/2021/08/13/migrant-encounters-at-u-s-mexico-border-are-at-a-21-year-high.

Hackman, M. (2022, May 20). Federal judge blocks Biden administration from ending Title 42. *Wall Street Journal*. Retrieved from: https://www.wsj.com/articles/federal-judge-blocks-biden-administration-from-ending-title-42-11653081923.

Hackman, M., & Parti, T. (2022, April 27). Facing heat from all sides, Mayorkas defends border policies. *Wall Street Journal*. Retrieved from: https://www.wsj.com/articles/facing-heat-from-all-sides-mayorkas-to-defend-border-policies-11651060800.

Huber, C. (2021, April 7). Texas AG Paxton sues Biden administration, claiming "failure to secure the border." Spectrumlocalnews.com. Retrieved from: https://spectrumlocalnews.com/tx/south-texas-el-paso/news/2021/04/07/texas-ag-paxton-sues-biden-administration--claiming--failure-to-secure-the-border-.

Huber, C. (2022, April 28). Texas AG Ken Paxton sues Biden administration over border for 11th time. Spectrumlocalnews.com. Retrieved from: https://spectrumlocalnews.com/tx/south-texas-el-paso/news/2022/04/28/texas-ag-ken-paxton-sues-biden-administration-over-border-for-11th-time-.

Lopez, B. (2022, January 26). Gov. Greg Abbott taps into parent anger to fuel reelection campaign. *Texas Tribune*. Retrieved from: https://www.texastribune.org/2022/01/26/greg-abbott-parental-bill-of-rights.

McGee, K. (2022, May 5). Gov. Greg Abbott says federal government should cover cost of educating undocumented students in Texas public schools. *Texas Tribune*. Retrieved from: https://www.texastribune.org/2022/05/05/greg-abbott-plyler-doe-education/amp.

Sullivan, E., & Jordan, M. (2021, October 22). Illegal border crossings, driven by pandemic and natural disasters, soar to record high. *New York Times*. Retrieved from: https://www.nytimes.com/2021/10/22/us/politics/border-crossings-immigration-record-high.html.

U.S. Citizenship and Immigration Services. (2022). Consideration of Deferred Action for Childhood Arrivals (DACA). Retrieved from: https://www.uscis.gov/DACA.

References for Educating Migrants in Texas—Enthusiasts

Lopez, B. (2022, January 26). Gov. Greg Abbott taps into parent anger to fuel reelection campaign. *Texas Tribune*. Retrieved from: https://www.texastribune.org/2022/01/26/greg-abbott-parental-bill-of-rights.

Texas Association of School Boards. (2018). Student immigration issues in Texas Public Schools. Retrieved from: https://www.tasb.org/services/legal-services/tasb-school-law-esource/students/documents/student_immigration_issues.aspx.

Winter, C. (2017, August 21). A Supreme Court case 35 years ago yields a supply of emboldened DACA students today. Apmreports.org. Retrieved from: https://www.apmreports.org/story/2017/08/21/plyler-doe-daca-students.

References for Educating Migrants in Texas—Skeptics

Children at Risk. (2022). PK-12 education. Childrenatrisk.org. Retrieved from: https://childrenatrisk.org/education.

Donaldson, E., Richman, T., & Smith, C. (2022, April 20). Too big to fail? Texas' largest teacher prep program riddled with problems, state finds. *Dallas Morning News*. Retrieved from: https://www.dallasnews.com/news/education/2022/04/20/too-big-to-fail-texas-largest-teacher-prep-program-riddled-with-problems-state-finds.

Mandelbaum, R. (2021, July 23). This is what happens to child migrants found alone at the border, from the moment they cross into the US until age 18. Theconversation.com. Retrieved from: https://theconversation.com/this-is-what-happens-to-child-migrants-found-alone-at-the-border-from-the-moment-they-cross-into-the-us-until-age-18-163205.

Mitchell, C. (2018, May 25). There are times when schools can't shield undocumented families. *Education Week*. Retrieved from: https://www.edweek.org/policy-politics/there-are-times-when-schools-cant-shield-undocumented-families/2018/05#:~:text=Under%20federal%20guidance%2C%20K%2D12,differently%20than%20U.S.%20citizen%20students.

About the Author

Gerard Giordano recently served as professor at the University of North Florida. He has written previous books about the impact parents have on schools. All of them have been published by Rowman & Littlefield.

www.ingramcontent.com/pod-product-compliance
Lightning Source LLC
Chambersburg PA
CBHW020738230426
43665CB00009B/477